Why We Fought

WHY WE FOUGHT

FORGING AMERICAN OBLIGATIONS
IN WORLD WAR II

ROBERT B. WESTBROOK

Smithsonian Books
Washington

Grateful acknowledgment is made for permission to reprint the following:

"In the Mirror of the Enemy: Japanese Political Culture and the Peculiarities of American Patriotism in World War II," in John Bodnar, ed., *Bonds of Affection: Americans Define Their Patriotism* (Princeton, NJ: Princeton University Press, 1996). © 1996 by Princeton University Press.

"Fighting for the American Family: Private Interests and Political Obligation in World War II," in Richard Wightman Fox and T. J. Jackson Lears, eds., *The Power of Culture: Critical Essays in American History* (Chicago: University of Chicago Press, 1993). © 1993 by The University of Chicago. All rights reserved.

"'I Want a Girl, Just Like the Girl That Married Harry James': American Women and the Problem of Political Obligation in World War II," *American Quarterly* 42 (1990): 587–614. © 1990 American Studies Association.

"The Responsibility of Peoples: Dwight Macdonald and the Holocaust," in Sanford Pinsker and Jack Fischel, eds., *America and the Holocaust*, special issue of *Holocaust Studies Annual* 1 (1983): 35–68. © The Penkeville Publishing Company, Greenwood, Florida.

Copy editor: Craig Triplett

Production editor: Joanne Reams

Designer: Brian Barth

Library of Congress Cataloging-in-Publication Data

Westbrook, Robert B. (Robert Brett), 1950–

   Why we fought : forging American obligations in World War II / Robert B. Westbrook.

    p. cm.

   Includes bibliographical references and index.

   ISBN 1-58834-130-5 (alk. paper)

    1. World War, 1939–1945—Social aspects—United States. 2. United States—Social conditions—1933–1945. 3. United States—Politics and government—1933–1945.

   4. Patriotism—United States—History—20th century. 5. Political culture—United States—History—20th century. I. Title.

E806.W4545   2004

940.53'73—dc22   2004041670

British Library Cataloguing-in-Publication Data is available

Manufactured in the United States of America

10 09 08 07 06 05 04   1 2 3 4 5

♾ The paper used in this publication meets the minimum requirements of the American National Standard for Information Sciences—Permanence of Paper for Printed Library Materials ANSI Z39.48-1992.

For my parents, whose war it was

There is no such thing possible as an ethical philosophy dogmatically made up in advance. We all help to determine the content of ethical philosophy so far as we contribute to the race's moral life. In other words, there can be no final truth in ethics any more than in physics, until the last man has had his experience and said his say. In the one case as in the other, however, the hypotheses which we now make while waiting, and the acts to which they prompt us, are among the indispensable conditions which determine what that "say" shall be.

—William James, "The Moral Philosopher and the Moral Life."

Contents

Acknowledgments

I am grateful to Jeffrey Hardwick for suggesting that I collect these essays for republication, and then for convincing his colleagues at Smithsonian Books that it was worth doing. Nicole Sloan, Joanne Reams, Emily Sollie, and Brian Barth of Smithsonian Books were most helpful as well. Craig Triplett proved a fine copy editor.

For assistance with the illustrations, I thank Jemal Creary, Corbis Images; Diane Kaplan, Manuscripts and Archives Department, Yale University; Rona Tuccillo, Getty Images; and Martha Smith and Michael Malerk, Photography Services of the University of Rochester Medical School. Special thanks to Thomas Rockwell for allowing me again to reproduce the three Norman Rockwell paintings. My appreciation as well is extended to those corporate executives who permitted the reproduction of advertisements.

Some of the original versions of these chapters came bearing thanks to those who helped me work out the arguments. Let me repeat them here to Jean-Christophe Agnew, Betsy Blackmar, John Bodnar, Richard Fox, Deborah Gorham, Macgregor Knox, Gary Kulik,

Chris Lehmann, Roy Rosenzweig, Solomon Wank, Stewart Weaver, and Suzanne Wolk. The essay on Dwight Macdonald bears heavily the mark of my longtime friend Robert Cummings. Macdonald once told Bob that Bob knew more about his life and work than he did himself, and he was right.

Undergraduates at Yale and the University of Rochester provided a willing and able audience for the half-formed thoughts out of which these essays emerged. They have been among my most astute critics. Two Yale students merit special mention. I first began to put together my arguments about the mobilization of private obligations while advising the senior essay of Mindy Rosenbaum in 1984. Mindy and I did not always agree on these matters, but we worked things out, and I learned as much from her as she from me. Karla Goldman's senior essay on New York intellectuals and the Holocaust, which I advised in 1982, made me think about Macdonald's unique place in that circle, and the arguments of the first part of the essay on him are heavily indebted not only to this fine essay, but to several stimulating conversations with her.

My wife, Shamra Westbrook, was skeptical of the virtues of momentarily setting aside John Dewey for Betty Grable, but she came around and proved, as always, an indispensable reader. It was less I than Christopher Lasch who changed her mind. This is but one of many forever unpaid debts to him.

My parents, J. C. and Nancy Westbrook, not only provided pivotal documents but afforded ample inspiration to solve the puzzles they presented. I am especially delighted to have a book such as this to dedicate to them.

Why We Fought

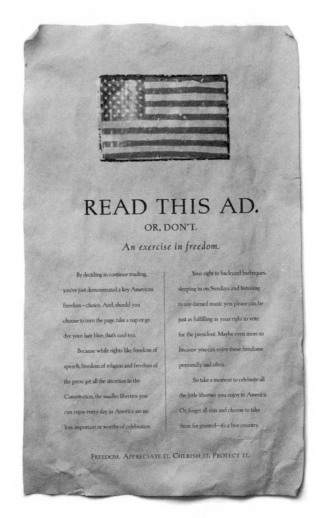

The mobilization of private commitments so prominent in World War II continues. Ad-Council public service announcement, *New York Times*, 15 July 2003.

Introduction

World War II and the Social History
of the American Moral Imagination

The essays collected in this book reflect what has been a somewhat serendipitous coincidence of two keen interests: a concrete, substantive, personal interest in the American experience of World War II and a more abstract, methodological, theoretical interest in fostering a union of history, moral philosophy, and political theory. For me, this has been a happy coincidence of concerns, and with these essays I hope to convince readers that it might be so for them as well.

For my parents, as for many such Americans who came of age in the 1940s, World War II was the world-historical event that most profoundly shaped their experience. Though the Great Depression, which they weathered as teenagers, had a great impact on their sensibilities, it was the war that most altered the trajectory of their lives.

Indeed, were it not for the war, my parents might never have met. Born in the still decidedly distinctive regions of the upper Midwest and the upper South, they took part in the tremendous geographical mobility that the war generated. My father, raised in Arkansas, was an enlisted man in the Army Air Force and served in Alaska, where he happily suffered no wounds beyond frostbite. In 1943 he was transferred to Santa Maria, California, into a unit training jet pilots. My mother, raised in Minnesota, left college when the war began and worked near his base as a secretary to an Air Force surgeon. My parents met in 1945 and married in 1946. Urged by my mother to take full advantage of the opportunities afforded by the GI Bill, my father enrolled in 1947 at the University of Denver and graduated three years later with a degree in business administration. He then began a long and distinguished career in western Colorado with the raw materials division of the Atomic Energy Commission, a government agency spawned by the wartime development of the atomic bomb. My mother, like many women of her generation who had found rewarding work during the war, devoted herself thereafter to raising the sort of family for which the war had been fought. The "lived theory" that I describe in these essays is the lived theory of my upbringing—and a not at all uncommon story.

I came of age myself in the 1960s, a decade given to intergenerational political conflict. Such conflict was very much a part of my experience, but I emerged from it with a fresh respect for my parents and a growing interest in knowing more about the circumstances in which they had forged their early lives and in applying my skills as a historian to this task. I gave World War II a prominent place in courses I was teaching on recent American history, and about twenty years ago I began to offer lecture courses and seminars strictly on the American experience of the war. These essays emerged, in large part, from that teaching.

At the same time, I was trying to find a way to combine my work as a historian with an abiding interest in political theory and moral philosophy that I had developed as an undergraduate and expanded when I wrote a book on the American philosopher John Dewey.[1] I was teaching at the time in the American Studies Program at Yale University, which proved the perfect setting in which to undertake this project. At this time—the early 1980s—American cultural history was beginning to flourish, and faculty and graduate students at Yale were making signal contributions to the field. It was an extraordinarily exciting place to work, and I tried to take full advantage of the opportunities it presented.

Cultural history was then and remains an ill-defined field, and I suspect that is one reason so many scholars have found it so attractive. It is the sort of undisciplined discipline where one can easily break with convention because it has so few of them. One consequence of this latitudinarianism is that a variety of interdisciplinary marriages have been arranged under cultural history's rubric. The best publicized of these engagements have witnessed historians in search of past *mentalités* courting anthropology and literary academics in quest of a "new historicism" romancing history (or at least Michel Foucault).[2] I was interested in an interdisciplinary cultural history somewhat outside the mainstream of contemporary "cultural studies," one that would bring together history and ethics (broadly conceived to include social and political theory) to help me to better understand what anthropologist Clifford Geertz nicely termed the "social history of the moral imagination." Not many people were doing this sort of work, but I took heart from exemplars such as Michael Walzer and Thomas Haskell.[3]

On several occasions, I taught an undergraduate seminar titled

"The Social History of the American Moral Imagination since 1945," in which we considered events and issues—such as atomic warfare, the civil rights movement, the war in Vietnam, abortion, affirmative action, environmental protection, and nuclear disarmament—that had moved the American people to open ethical debate. In a session on the military draft and draft resistance, we read some essays that Walzer had written during the Vietnam War on the "obligation to die for the state." In these essays, Walzer laid out the difficulties that liberal states have in arguing that such an obligation is *political*, forcing them to rely instead on essentially private moral obligations to mobilize their populations for war.[4]

At the same time, I was teaching a lecture course on recent American cultural history. I began the course with a slide show linking my own quite ordinary family's historical experience with the broader events and larger social forces that we would be examining in the course. With the evidence from my own family archives I hoped to encourage students to make similar connections between history and their family biographies. One of the documents I used was a wartime photograph of my mother, which, as students delightedly pointed out, was a homemade pin-up. In one of those unbidden flashes of insight that come all too infrequently, I connected Walzer's argument with the pin-up of my mother, and I began to formulate the hypothesis that pin-ups might have been more than cheesecake; they might show how liberal states, such as the United States in World War II, mobilized the private obligations of their citizens for war. I thus plunged into the admittedly pleasing world of Betty Grable and Rita Hayworth and wrote the third of these essays.

In doing this article, I began to get excited about doing more work in the history of what might best be called "popular political theory," a history of American political thought that centers on "ordinary" people or at least on people who are not intellectuals by conventional definition. Such history argues that just because most citizens are not political philosophers does not mean that they do not on occasion advance significant theoretical arguments or that we should not subject these arguments to the same scrutiny that we give to those of intellectual elites. Philosopher Michael Sandel nicely stated the rationale for this conviction in a lecture I heard shortly after I began teaching at the University of Rochester in 1986:

> Our practices and institutions are embodiments of theory. We could hardly describe our political life, much less engage in it, without recourse to a language laden with theory. Political institutions are not simply instruments that implement ideas independently conceived; they are themselves embodiments of ideas. We live some theory—all the time. . . . If theory never keeps its distance, but inhabits the world from the start, we may find a clue to our condition in the theory that we live. Attending to the theory implicit in our public life may help diagnose our political condition. It may also reveal that the predicament of American democracy resides not only in the gap between our ideals and institutions, but also within the ideals themselves, and within the self-image our public life reflects.

This view points toward a critical cultural history of American politics that aims, as Sandel says, "to identify the public philosophy implicit in our practices and institutions, and to show how tensions in the philosophy show up in the practice." Historians who pursue this task must be prepared to find political theory not only among political theorists and politicians, but in some unusual places—even in pin-ups of Betty Grable.[5]

This interdisciplinary project assumes that there need not be a sharp divide between the historical study of the ethical imagination of those whom we call philosophers over those we do not. Just as one can better understand the work of philosophers by understanding the life they share with nonphilosophers, so clues to the assumptions and tensions in the thinking of nonphilosophers can be found in the work of philosophers, where they are often more elaborated. Just as the study of preeminent intellectuals can benefit from an understanding of the larger culture in which they are embedded, so too can the investigation of the reflective life of less-articulate men and women profit from an awareness of the concerns of those who have made it their business to engage more explicitly with the conundrums of the moral life. If the history of popular political theory finds its documents in strange places, it finds many of the best questions to pose to these documents in the work of philosophers, as I hope the essays that follow will suggest.

Over the course of the last ten years or so, I have come to recognize that my attraction to the social history of the American moral imagination and to the role of history in moral inquiry more generally drew on my sympathetic engagement with the thinking of American pragmatists such as William James, John Dewey, and Richard Rorty, and it meshed with my participation in the revival of pragmatism that Rorty initiated in the early 1980s. For pragmatists, as neopragmatist Elizabeth Anderson has said,

> empirically grounded knowledge and forms of understanding bear
> upon the justification of ethical principles themselves. The most important source of empirical knowledge relevant to ethical justification
> comes from our experiences in living out the lives our ethical principles
> prescribe for us. We might find life in accordance with the principles we
> think are valid to be deeply unsatisfactory, to pose problems that are intolerable and irresolvable in terms of those very principles. Or we might
> find lives lived in accordance with fundamentally different principles to
> be profoundly attractive or appealing.[6]

Pragmatists thus tend to be deeply interested in the portraits of moral lives that those in the human sciences can offer them, and those engaged in humanistic and social scientific inquiry who offer such portraits contribute invaluably to moral inquiry, as pragmatists understand it. The pragmatist, as Anderson concludes, "urges us to view social, scientific, humanistic, and ethical inquiry as interconnected aspects of a joint enterprise."[7]

The interdisciplinary moral inquiry that pragmatism authorizes finds particular riches in what one might call the "narrative disciplines"—ethnography, literary criticism, and history, for example—since they collect and analyze those stories that illuminate the moral life. A wide-ranging and open-ended moral inquiry convinced of the evidentiary value of such stories requires scholars—ethnographers, historians, and critics—capable of journeying for a time to a "boundary" that Robert Orsi has so eloquently described: "an in-between orientation, located at the intersection of self and other, at the boundary between one's own moral universe and the moral world of the other . . . ground that belongs completely neither to oneself or to the other but that has come into being between them, precisely because of the meeting of the two." It is here alone, as Orsi says, that "one comes to know something about the other and about oneself through relationship with the other."[8] A particularly fraught boundary when, as I say, the "others" in question include one's parents, but a necessary place to stand in any case.

Researching the Betty Grable article convinced me that pin-ups were not the only evidence of a popular political theory of obligation at work in American culture during wartime, and that World War II was a particularly good war in which to study it. As a "total war," it mobilized most of the society and, as a consequence, the number of people who worried over issues of obligation was broad and diverse. World War II was also the first American war to follow the consolidation of mass culture and social science, and as a result I had a wealth of material to draw on: advertisements, movies, radio programs, photographs, mass circulation newspapers and magazines, and reports of researchers who asked people what they thought about the war. Also, because the operations of the Creel Committee in charge of American propaganda during World War I had been widely criticized and because the public identified centralized propaganda agencies with the totalitarian enemy, propaganda production in World War II was more decentralized and much was left to private initiative. Thus the common themes evident in this prescriptive material perhaps reflect more widely shared attitudes than they would if it had been produced by a single bureaucracy. Because the vast majority of Americans regarded World War II as a just war also simplified matters somewhat, since people's thinking about why they should fight for their country at all—the issue that interested me most—was not complicated by their need to consider why they should fight for their country in this particular war.[9]

My wider research into the theory of obligation at work in wartime American political culture is evident in the first two essays. After examining sources such as advertisements, movies, popular journalism, and other available evidence of felt as well as prescribed obligations, I concluded that I could more broadly state the argument I had advanced in the pin-up article. Consistent with its liberal-democratic underpinnings, popular thinking about obligation to the US war effort during World War II manifested the difficulties that liberalism has in advancing a compelling argument for a political obligation to go to war, even a war as just as the struggle against the Axis powers. Liberal arguments appealed instead to abstract ethical principles that transcended political obligations to the United States, and they appealed to private, nonpolitical moral obligations—above all, those to the family. Strictly speaking, Americans in World War II were not instructed to fight, work, and die for their country. More often than not, they were urged to wage war as fathers, mothers, husbands, wives, lovers, sons, daughters, and consumers—not as citizens. More often than not, I say, but not always. We can also learn much, I suggest, by looking at exceptional, nonliberal arguments such as those advanced in Norman Rockwell's extraordinary painting, *Freedom of Speech*.

My argument is inherently comparative. If nonliberal states such as Japan drew heavily on similar arguments during the war to mobilize its population, then my claim for the peculiarities of American popular political culture and its roots in liberalism would be dubious. But nonliberal states, given to thicker, more organic conceptions of citizenship and national identity, found arguing for a particularistic, political obligation to fight a war much easier than the United States did. Indeed, as I argue in the first essay, American observers during the war often contrasted the thin, liberal universalism of American political culture with the thick, collectivist particularism of the Japanese enemy. Americans who regarded themselves as citizens of an aggregated "state of families" viewed the organic Japanese "family state" with contempt and, occasionally, with wistful respect. Here liberal theory not only informed American conceptions of "why we fight" but also became itself an object of loyalty.

I have made a few, mostly modest revisions in the first three essays to eliminate repetition and stitch them together. I have also made one important substantive change. In the initial versions, I referred to private obligations, commitments, and *interests*, but I have found that, despite my best efforts to stress the typically moral (if not political) and other-regarding nature of these interests, some readers have interpreted the term as meaning *self*-interested, even selfish, pursuits. So I have taken the opportunity to make myself even clearer, and I now refer strictly to *obligations* and *commitments*.

The final essay in the book was written first, and until I began to assemble this collection, I had not considered it of a piece with the others. And in some respects it is not. It focuses not on popular political theory but on an intellectual, Dwight Macdonald, whose views were both unpopular and uncomfortable. It also centers on an event, the Holocaust, that was (alas) not an important part of the thinking of American policymakers and most of their constituents during the war. Yet, like Rockwell's painting, I think a consideration of Macdonald's reflections on "the responsibility of peoples" belongs in this collection not because it was typical of American thinking about political and moral obligation, but precisely because it was not.

While Americans debated about "why we fight," Macdonald offered a darker prospect, the claim that the question was properly phrased in the passive voice: "why we are fought." That is, while attacking the efforts by many to hold the whole of the German people responsible for the Holocaust, he concluded unhappily that, for most Germans, their lack of responsibility was attributable not to their resistance to the Nazis but to the erosion in Germany of the very conditions for responsible action. And, even more troubling, he claimed that this erosion was at work in every modern, industrialized state. "Modern society," he contended, "has become so tightly organized, so rationalized and routinized that, it has the character of a mechanism which grinds on without human consciousness or control."[10] Debates about political obligation, Macdonald argued, presumed the active agency, consent, and authority of ordinary citizens, which was nearly absent not only in Germany but in the United States as well. "Not for centuries," he remarked, "have individuals been at once so powerless to influence what is done by the national collectivities to which they belong, and at the same time so generally held responsible for what is done by those collectivities." A critic not only of Nazi and Soviet crimes but of the American terror bombing that culminated at Hiroshima and Nagasaki, Macdonald found that the world had become "a complicated and terrifying place, in which un-understood social forces move men puppetlike to perform terrible acts."[11]

Macdonald's argument was not without its shortcomings and exaggerations, and I endeavor to point these out. Yet I still think sociologist Daniel Bell was correct to say that Macdonald was one of the few during the war who "was aware of and insistently kept calling attention to, changes that were taking place in moral temper, the depths of which we still incompletely realize."[12] Unlike Betty Grable and Norman Rockwell, Macdonald understood that absent the sort of democracy portrayed in *Freedom of Speech*, ordinary citizens were less obliged than coerced to risk their lives for modern states. In relations between individual citizens and such states, "precisely because in this sphere the individual is most powerless in reality, do his rulers make their greatest efforts to present the State not only as an instrument for *his* purposes but as an extension of *his* personality."[13]

But absent robust democracy, I think liberalism is better than the alternative in time of war—if not for those who would send citizens into battle, then at least for those who will do the dying. I fear this conviction is not as evident in these essays as it should be, so I state it firmly here. Better, that is, to be subject to a state that has difficulty making the case that it is the instrument of our purposes—let alone an extension of our personalities—when it puts our lives or those of our loved ones at stake. If Macdonald exposed a foreboding side to the responsibility of peoples during World War II that Betty Grable's smile obscured, she gave the lie to his too-ready dimming of the differences between Germany and the United States. If we cannot decide whether to go to war as democratic citizens, better to make this decision as parents, children, lovers, and friends. Then, at least, our purposes will be our own.

In the Mirror of the Enemy

Japanese Political Culture and the
Peculiarities of American Patriotism

There is nothing like a war to concentrate the minds of citizens on the meaning of patriotism, national identity, and political obligation. When our country is at war and we ask "why we fight," we seek to understand not only the aims of a particular war, but also, in a deeper and more general sense, just what binds us to (or alienates us from) our nation-state. Wartime is one of those rare occasions during which the political theory implicit in our institutions and practices becomes explicit and a widely shared concern. In the middle of a war, we recognize as we often do not on less crisis-ridden occasions that, as Michael Sandel has put it, "we live some theory—all the time."[1]

Gen. Douglas MacArthur meeting with defeated
Japanese emperor Hirohito at the US Embassy
in Tokyo, 27 September 1945.

Sometimes we find ourselves at war with an enemy living quite a different theory, and this discovery sharpens our sense of the peculiarities of our own theory. The more alien the political culture of an enemy nation is, the more it may goad us to self-consciousness and the more theoretical such self-reflection may become. In such a situation, we may well not only make theoretical arguments for "why we fight" but also think in second-order fashion about our political theory itself. In the face of an enemy we find especially difficult to understand, our thinking can take a "metatheoretical" turn. The more remote the thinking of our enemy, the more likely that our lived political theory will not just inform our patriotism but will itself become a mark of our national identity.

Arguably, no enemy has ever afforded Americans a more alien political culture against which to measure themselves than Japan did during World War II.[2] This view, at least, was widely held at the time. During the war, Hitler seemed far more explicable to most American commentators than the foe in the Pacific. Americans would do well, the editors of *Fortune* warned typically in 1942, not to allow superficial similarities between the Nazi and Japanese regimes to obscure the wider moral gulf that divided the United States from the Asian enemy. "Whereas Nazi terrorism is the result of a conscious, calculated science of annihilation, on the excuse of the ends justifying the means, and is backed up at every step by long-winded moralizings, the Japanese brand is unhampered by ethical claptrap." Or, at least, the editors conceded, unhampered by familiar ethical claptrap:

> The unfathomable combined influence of Buddhism, Confucianism, and the primitive Shinto on the Japanese has reduced the importance of the individual to little or nothing. The ancient compulsions for unlimited self-sacrifice, the exaltation of the community over the individual,

of rulers over law, and of death over life, have numbed the sense of intellectual and moral discrimination and made the Japanese indifferent to suffering—his own or others.

The Nazis, this argument implied, could easily be judged evil in conventional terms, but the Japanese operated beyond American—that is, Western—conventions of good and evil. The Nazis were bad Germans, to be judged by standards Americans shared with good Germans, but the Japanese were another matter. They were, as a people, living in a different ethical universe. Americans could not distinguish between good and evil Japanese because good and evil did not mean the same things to the Japanese as they did to Americans (and good Germans). Hence, *Fortune* concluded, war with Japan afforded an especially difficult moral challenge. "We must be prepared," the magazine said, "to fight everywhere and anywhere—on the lofty and dangerous terrain of philosophy and ethics, no less than on the conventional battlegrounds of classic strategy."[3]

This essay analyzes the battle Americans waged on this lofty and dangerous terrain, focusing on their attempts to understand and describe Japanese political culture, particularly the conceptions of political obligation and patriotism embedded in it. But I am less interested in these descriptions themselves than in how they served implicitly, and sometimes explicitly, to help Americans understand their own conceptions of political obligation and patriotism. For behind efforts to understand "why they fight" lay an attempt to grasp better the decidedly different reasons for "why we fight."

Nature's Nation
Since the founding of the United States, many have contended that the dominant conception of American national identity is rooted in

classical liberalism and is, when compared with other nationalisms, a most peculiar notion. For most nations, as Samuel P. Huntington has argued, "national identity is the product of a long process of historical evolution involving common ancestors, common experiences, common ethnic background, common language, common culture, and usually common religion." But American civic identity has lacked such ascriptive elements and has required only a subscription to the ideals of liberal democracy: "liberty, equality, individualism, democracy, and the rule of law under a constitution." American nationalism, peculiarly voluntaristic and creedal, is rendered even more peculiar by the fact that the ideals of the "American Creed" are often said (despite the adjective) to embody universal, even natural, rights. Thus, even though nationalism would seem by definition to claim a kind of particularity, American nationalism in its liberal formulation argues somewhat paradoxically for a nationalism that transcends particularity. The United States is less a nation among nations than an exceptional place where human beings can enjoy those rights and liberties to which they are entitled, whatever their particular identities may be. America is "Nature's nation."[4]

One important consequence of this liberal understanding of American national identity is a thin sense of political community and a set of inadequate and, to some critics, incoherent and wholly unpersuasive liberal arguments for political obligations to the national state. Political obligation would seem to require moral and affective ties to a particular political community, but liberals have found such ties difficult to establish within the confines of their individualistic, voluntaristic, contractual, and instrumental understanding of the relationship of citizens to the state. However, liberal nationalism, oxymoron though it may be, has often served as a bulwark against the terrors that the deep particularism of other nationalisms has generated both within and without national borders.[5]

War, the greatest test of political obligation, has put a liberal nation such as the United States at something of an ideological disadvantage in mobilizing its citizens to fight. Unable to draw on the strong arguments for political obligation available to the leaders of nonliberal nations, American political leaders have often attempted to mobilize their citizenry with appeals to ethical values transcending any particular political community (the supposedly universal ideals of liberal democracy) or to nonpolitical private moral obligations. The state appears not as the embodiment of a particular political community but as either the guarantor of *human* rights or the protector of an essentially *private* sphere. Appeals to transnational values (such as Franklin Roosevelt's "Four Freedoms") and nonpolitical obligations (such as those of men to women and parents to children) were preeminent during World War II. This chapter will deal with the first of these appeals; the two that follow focus on the second.

Few contemporary historians continue to contend, as some once did, that American national identity is solely founded on liberalism. As Rogers Smith has effectively argued, liberal conceptions of American national identity and citizenship have always competed with more particularistic republican and ethnocultural traditions that have afforded, for better or worse, a thicker sense of political community and more compelling arguments for political obligation. Americans have in war and peace used each of these traditions and often articulated various amalgams of the three. Moreover, during the late nineteenth and early twentieth centuries, an ethnocultural understanding of American national identity was arguably hegemonic and not terribly different from the nastier nationalisms seldom identified with the United

States. But, as Smith concedes, by World War II the liberal tradition again held the upper hand, though the other traditions were not without significance. Thus, Americans scrutinized Japanese political culture largely through the lens of liberalism.[6]

The Japanese Anthill

In the wake of Pearl Harbor, American newspapers and magazines not only provided reports from the battlefront but also occasionally published feature articles that sought to explain Japanese nationalism to their readers. *Fortune* even devoted most of two issues to an effort to understand what its editors termed the "paradoxes of behavior that have twisted the Japanese mind for centuries." Many of these features were written by journalists and scholars such as Hugh Byas, Gustav Eckstein, Karl Löwith, Helen Mears, Joseph Newman, Willard Price, and Otto Tolischus, people who had spent time in Japan before the war, and former ambassador to Japan Joseph Grew regularly contributed to this literature as well. Government agencies such as the Office of War Information employed experts, such as anthropologist Ruth Benedict, to study the Japanese character, and military intelligence officers provided soldiers and sailors with lectures and pamphlets on the political culture of the enemy. Documentary filmmakers such as Frank Capra not only instructed Americans in their own war aims but also provided them with such films as *Know Your Enemy—Japan* (1945) and *The Enemy Japan* (1943), designed to instruct them in the ways of their adversary. Thus, during the war a relatively popular discourse on Japanese political culture became a significant feature of American public life.[7]

Although those Americans who sought to explain Japanese nationalism to their fellow citizens were not without their differences of opinion, their work did share a handful of themes. At the core of this American wartime commentary on Japanese national identity was the perception of the Japanese as an extraordinarily "collectivist" people, a people devoid of individuality—"photographic prints off the same negative," as Capra put it in *Know Your Enemy—Japan.* "From childhood up," Willard Price told the readers of *National Geographic* magazine, the Japanese "are taught that the individual is of slight importance, . . . Japan has no rugged individualism. She has a rugged collectivism." According to *Fortune*, "in their individual lives, the Japanese have little opportunity for self-expression, simply because they do not exist as individuals at all. They exist as a unit of a family, as an object of the state, as a part of a group to which they are always subordinate."[8]

Such collectivism, commentators argued, was reflected in the extraordinary solidarity among the Japanese people. "It would be harder in Japan to cut between rulers and people than in any other country in the world," argued Gustav Eckstein. "Emperor, military leaders, and people will rise or go down to defeat together." Unlike Germany, Japan had not sent legions of dissenting emigrants to Allied shores. "The difference between German sheep and Nazi wolves is easily exposed," remarked Hugh Byas. "It is demonstrated by the testimony of many eminent Germans who have fled from the tyranny which they denounce. No such evidence can be produced in the case of Japan."[9]

Amidst this solidarity, Americans discerned a troubling, unreflective loyalty to the state. The Japanese, Byas noted, are "steeped in an ethical training which makes loyalty to country its deity." For those so trained, "national unity is an end in itself. The state says to them, 'Thou shalt have no other gods beside me.'" As William Henry Chamberlain saw it, "The slogan, 'My country, right or wrong,' would be alien to a Japanese—he simply could not conceive that his country could be wrong." In the fall of 1945, the Navy instructed American sailors on their way to Japan that "the words the Japanese hears from the cradle to the grave are 'obey,' 'obey,' 'obey.'"[10]

American critics searching for the peculiarities of Japanese nationalism commonly singled out several features of Japanese political culture for comment: (1) the claims for the emperor's divinity; (2) the familial ideology in which worship of the emperor was embedded; and (3) the "fanaticism" this ideology produced among Japanese soldiers wedded to it.

American readers and American troops preparing to face the Japanese were repeatedly told the story of the mythic descent of Emperor Hirohito from the sun goddess Amaterasu, who sent her son to rule over the Japanese before the dawn of recorded history. They were alerted to the fact that this myth and the religion of State Shinto or "emperor-worship" that grew up around it constituted an "invented tradition" that dated from the Meiji Restoration of 1867 and the subsequent efforts of Meiji elites to develop an ideology with which to forge national unity. Nonetheless, most American commentators argued that the Japanese masses firmly believed in their emperor's divinity and that less credulous Japanese elites at least kept up the appearance of belief so that the masses would continue their worship. As the editors of the *Christian Century* described this "blasphemous theory":

> The Japanese constitution declares that the emperor is "sacred and inviolable." His office is not an organ of the state. The line of Japanese emperors, "unbroken from ages eternal" since the first emperor descended from Amaterasu Omikami, the sun goddess, existed before the nation and gives the state its being. The only powers exercised by the people, according to the theory on which the government of Nippon is built, are those derived from the emperor. In nearly two thousand years, the history of Western nations affords no parallel to the powers claimed by this ruler.

The theory of the divine right of kings had not half the sweeping presumption of the thesis on which the Japanese god emperor bases his authority. While there have been times when the point was not pressed with the relentless fury now in evidence, since 1931 it has not been possible for anyone in the Sunrise Kingdom to express doubt that the emperor is a god, entitled to blind and absolute obedience from his subjects, who are themselves demi-gods by reason of their relationship to him.[11]

Worshipping the emperor sustained a powerful form of patriotism, which was its intended purpose. Strictly speaking, Chamberlain observed, "emperor-worship, as practiced in Japan, is not a religious cult, as we understand the term, but rather a mood of super-patriotism, of a salute to the flag with an added element of religious awe and sanction." The emperor was, above all, "a bond of national unity."[12]

Much of the power of the emperor's cult, American commentators argued, lay in the manner in which it was bound up with Japanese loyalty to the family. "Very few Japanese," Chamberlain reported, "conceive themselves outside the framework of the family, with its authority and obligations for the stronger and more successful and its dependence and limited protection for the poorer and weaker." Moreover, the Japanese state was conceived ideologically as a "family state," with the obligations of citizenship modeled on filial obligation. The nation was an extended familial national pyramid with the emperor at its apex.[13] The emperor was not only divine; he was quite literally the "father" of his country. Military intelligence officers were instructed that

Japan is one big household, with the Emperor as its head, recipient of the filial piety and obedience traditional to the Japanese family. The Emperor is thus the basis of national unity in terms of religion and the family system. . . . And in theory, at least, this religious and unique quality operating in Japanese life makes for social solidarity, a sense of common welfare and mutual dependence, with a minimum of self-interest and strife such as characterizes ordinary nations.[14]

"The Japanese are still essentially a clan," Eckstein argued. "What material for a fanatic nationalism. What material for an army. Obedience is an instinct. Submission is nature."[15]

The Japanese notion of political obligation that attracted the most bewildered commentary from Americans was what they commonly termed the Japanese soldier's suicidal "fanaticism." Articles with titles such as "Perhaps He Is Human," "Japan's Fanatics in Uniform," "Japan's Soldiers: Unsoldierly Yet Fanatic," "Japan Digs In to Die," "Must We Butcher Them All?" and "These Nips Are Nuts" were regularly featured in popular magazines.[16] Again and again Americans read accounts such as this one by *Time* correspondent Robert Sherrod, who described Japanese soldiers choosing death and a "twisted" sense of honor over life and the shame of capture:

> The results of Jap fanaticism stagger the imagination. The very violence
> of the scene is incomprehensible to the Western mind. Here [Attu] groups
> of men had met their self-imposed obligation, to die rather than accept
> capture, by blowing themselves to bits. I saw one Jap sitting impaled on
> a bayonet which was stuck through his back, evidently by a friend. All
> the other suicides had chosen the grenade. Most of them simply held
> grenades against their stomachs or chests. The explosive charge blasted
> away the vital organs. Perhaps one in four held a grenade against his
> head. There were many headless Jap bodies between Massacre [Bay] and
> Chichagof [Harbor]. Sometimes the grenade split the head in half, leav
> ing the right face on one shoulder, the left face on the other.[17]

American reporters acknowledged that such suicidal behavior may well have resulted not only from ideological fanaticism but also the fears of Japanese soldiers that, as their superiors had told them, they would be horribly tortured by their American captors. But ideological explanations dominated the reporters' accounts. As *Time* put it, "Inside, the Japanese soldier is as tangled as the wires behind a telephone switchboard. From birth he has been taught the glory of dying for the Emperor. He knows what the manual says: 'To die participating in the supreme holy enterprise of mankind (war) must be the greatest glory and the height of exaltation.'"[18]

Efforts to explain Japanese patriotism varied. Occasionally, critics characterized the Japanese state with dehumanizing metaphors linking it to the social organization of collectivist insects such as ants and bees. "Japan is not a nation of individuals," Byas said, "but a hive of bees working, buzzing, and fighting collectively in defense of the hive." But despite the use of such racially inflected metaphors, popular literature on Japanese politics rarely explained Japanese political culture in strictly racial terms, and it was not marked by the overt racism that was so prominent in much anti-Japanese wartime propaganda.[19] More widespread were ahistorical, cultural explanations that built on the work of "culture and personality" anthropologists such as Ruth Benedict, Geoffrey Gorer, and Margaret Mead. These arguments often linked Japanese political culture to the nation's child-rearing practices, and they were sometimes popularized crudely in such reductionist arguments as one linking Japanese character and politics to severe toilet-training.[20]

But the preeminent explanation of Japanese political culture was less anthropological than historical, an argument that might perhaps best be termed the neomedieval or neofeudal thesis. According to this argument, Japan was a nation best understood as containing a mixture of modern and premodern elements in which the latter held the upper hand. After centuries of feudalism and isolation, when Japan opened to the West after confronting Commodore Matthew Perry's "black ships" in 1853, it took modernity in a carefully controlled embrace. The Meiji Restoration had not so much smashed hundreds of years of Japanese feudalism as revamped the nation as a peculiar, neo-feudal regime. "The ghost of feudalism," Douglas Haring observed, "still stalks Japan. One asks constantly whether it be a ghost at all." The supreme authority of the emperor was purely symbolic; Hirohito remained, as his predecessors had been, the instrument of elites who ruled through him. Once the tool of medieval shoguns, the emperor was now the vehicle of a "feudally minded military clique." The emperor, Joseph Newman said, was a "lonely man who plays the part of god behind his feudal prison in the heart of Tokyo."[21]

Everywhere in Japan, Haring remarked, one could find the "inner dreams" of feudalism encased in the trappings of modernity. Japanese soldiers armed with the latest weaponry nonetheless fancied themselves latter-day samurai and devoted themselves to an updated version of the code of Bushido, which required their unstinting, self-sacrificing devotion to the emperor. The apparent concessions Meiji elites and their successors had made to modern democracy—a popular electorate, a constitution, and parliamentary government—produced a false front, a "Potemkin democracy," thinly disguising an oppressive regime of elite rule, thought control, and terror. At the same time, the Japanese had embraced the Industrial Revolution, mimicking Western science and technical rationality and adopting "automobiles, western clothes, baseball, the movies, chewing gum, electric light, airplanes, machine guns, and battleships." In short, capitalism and modern technology had in Japan been grafted on to a recast yet ancient political order. As

Helen Mears summarized this argument, Japanese elites—now headed by the nation's military leaders—had produced a "fusion of the new and old Japan into a tightly meshed machine that can use the mechanical power of the Twentieth Century along with the dynamic of an ancient mythology."[22]

In nearly every narrative about the history of Japanese political culture, American commentators identified the long insular regime of Tokugawa feudalism (1603–1867) as the decisive period in Japanese national development. American accounts repeatedly argued that during the Tokugawa centuries the Japanese had missed the revolutions in thought and practice that had freed the West from the shackles of medievalism. As a Navy pamphlet put it, "From about 1600 to 1853, while the western world was experiencing the Renaissance, the Reformation, the growth of political and economic democracy, the effect of scientific inquiry and research—great movements and developments which have shaped our thinking and molded our behavior—Japan was locked up in complete isolation."[23]

Liberal democracy, on this account, was the boat on the progressive stream of modern political history that the Japanese had failed to catch, and nothing better explained the peculiar character of Japanese political culture than the liberal-democratic revolution that had not happened in Japan. The Tokugawa shoguns had chosen to close Japan off from Western influence at just the moment when the West had the most to offer. As a result of this misguided isolationism, *Fortune* argued, "the spirit and mind [of Japan] were frozen in the mold of medievalism." The tragedy of Japanese political history, the Navy pamphlet contended, was that "the complete elimination of all foreign influence, at a period when the western world was learning freedom, liberty, and the importance of developing individual personality, en-

abled the Japanese rulers to force the Japanese into a common mold."
The Japanese, a *New York Times* reporter remarked, had been left "outside modern thought," that is, outside liberal values and "all that has
gone into the making of the European and American mind with respect to group relations and the relations between constituted authority and the individual." Japanese political history, as these Americans
saw it, was not just different; it was anomalous—a case of arrested development measured against the liberal-democratic norm.[24]

American descriptions and explanations of Japanese political culture derived much of their persuasive power from using Japanese descriptions of their own culture. When the Japanese declared that they
were "100 million hearts beating as one," Americans took them at
their word, and Japanese manifestos such as the *Cardinal Principles of
the National Polity* (1937), *The Way of the Subject* (1941), and *The Way
of the Family* (1942), which described the Japanese state and Japanese
nationalism in much the same way that American critics did, were
widely cited. To impress upon his American readers the depths of Japanese statism, Hugh Byas, for example, quoted excerpts such as this
from a 1938 Japanese Department of Justice document:

> [All human beings] are born from the state, sustained by the state and
> brought up in the history and traditions of the state. Individuals can
> only exist as links in an infinite and vast chain of life called the state;
> they are links through whom the inheritance of ancestors is handed
> down to posterity, making possible continued growth and development
> in the future. . . . Individuals participate in the highest and greatest value
> when they serve the state as parts of it. The highest life for the Japanese
> subject is to offer himself in perfect loyalty to the Imperial throne so
> that he may participate in its glorious life.[25]

In this fashion, American reporters transformed positive Japanese self-descriptions of and prescriptions for communitarian solidarity into a negative portrait of a premodern state afflicted by irrational myths and a herdlike collectivism. As historian John Dower has said, Americans "accepted Japanese emphasis on the primacy of the group or collectivity at face value, and used this as prima facie evidence that the Japanese were closer to cattle or robots than to themselves."[26]

I have refrained from any attempt to judge the accuracy of American representations of Japanese political culture. But Dower, for one, has complained that these representations confused ideology and reality:

> It was not that the Japanese people were, in actuality, homogeneous and harmonious, devoid of individuality and thoroughly subordinated to the group, but rather that the Japanese ruling groups were constantly exhorting them to become so. Indeed, the government deemed it necessary to draft and propagate a rigid orthodoxy of this sort precisely because the ruling classes were convinced that a great many Japanese did not cherish the more traditional virtues of loyalty and filial piety under the emperor, but instead remained attracted to more democratic values and ideals. . . . In other words, what the vast majority of Westerners believed the Japanese to be coincided with what the Japanese ruling elites hoped they would become.[27]

Undoubtedly much could be said for this complaint, although I believe Dower underestimates both the sophistication of some of the American commentary and the degree to which orthodox ideology did indeed take hold among Japanese citizens and soldiers. But for my purposes, the issue may (thankfully) be left to Japanese historians. Even if Americans did construct a distorted and (negatively) idealized picture of Japanese political culture, this picture served effectively as a mirror that reflected their own (positively) idealized conceptions of political obligation and patriotism back to them.

Political Obligation, Thick and Thin

As I have noted, two arguments for "why we fight" were particularly significant in American public discourse during World War II. By and large representatives of the American state and other propagandists urged the nation's citizens to support the war effort for two reasons: to preserve the presumably universal human rights and liberties of liberal democracy that Axis aggression threatened; or to discharge a set of essentially private moral obligations to individuals and interests similarly threatened—commitments to families, children, parents, friends, and neighbors, and generally to an "American Way of Life," defined as a rich and rewarding private sphere of experience.[28] Both these arguments were "thin" arguments for political obligation because neither advocated obligations to a particular political community; at most, loyalty to the American state was conceived as an instrumental virtue, a means for discharging obligations that lay elsewhere. Strictly speaking, Americans were seldom asked to work, to fight, or to die for their country. Their leaders instructed them in obligations defined either as those transcending the particularity of the nation-state or those residing in a private, nonpolitical realm of particularity. In both cases, "thicker" Japanese conceptions of political obligation served as an effective foil to highlight the virtues of this anorectic, liberal nationalism.

"The Japanese challenge not only the power of the West," *Fortune* declared, "but its fundamental creeds." Above all, Japanese political culture was an affront to the liberal democratic values of liberty and equality that defined American civic identity. The American nation was founded in a revolutionary break with an oppressive state that threatened human rights and in the constitution of a new nation that would preserve them. As Americans saw it, the nation-state was properly conceived as a voluntary, contractual arrangement among free, rights-bearing individuals, designed above all to protect individual life and liberty and advance the pursuit of private happiness. The Japanese state, however, was designed to limit the freedom of ordinary men and women in the interests of a neofeudal elite. According to this idealized liberal argument, American patriotism was less loyalty to the American nation than loyalty to transcendent liberal principles of which that nation was the instrument. Japanese patriotism was unthinking loyalty to a state that violated these principles at every turn, a view any Japanese "fascist" would gladly confirm. Magazines like *Fortune* could readily find quotations from such figures as Baron Hiranuma expressing contempt for liberalism and its values. "No dust shall be allowed to becloud the radiance of the Imperial way," Hiranuma warned, "and what I call dust is represented by liberalism and individualism, which are both opposed to our traditional customs."[29]

By American lights then, most Japanese were less citizens than subjects. In the United States, the legitimacy of the state and political obligation rested in theory on popular consent rather than the "will of heaven," against which there could be no appeal. In America, citizens jealously guarded their freedom and granted the state only those powers that would render this freedom more secure. In Japan the power of the state rested not on the consent of the governed but on their unwavering obedience to a hierarchy of authorities. Cut off from the riches of the liberal tradition, the Japanese were "a people without a conception of their own slavery."[30]

For Americans national identity was secondary to "life, liberty, and the pursuit of happiness"; indeed, to be an American was to make national identity a means to pursue these universal values. But for the Japanese, a particularistic national identity seemed an end in itself, an end to which they appeared more than willing to sacrifice life, liberty, and happiness. Liberalism afforded a vision of a national state constituted by free individuals who preexisted the social contract that underlay their government; in the organic conception of state and society articulated by the Japanese, the state constituted its subjects, subjects who had no existence prior to or apart from their national family.

Americans found this thick, organic, self-constituting nationalism mystifying and even depraved. As Karl Löwith put it, with decided understatement, "It is difficult for us to understand why the ultimate values for the Japanese mind have never been 'life, liberty, and the pursuit of happiness,' but rather loyalty, a free disregard of life, and an honorable death." What made the suicidal behavior of Japanese soldiers so appalling to Americans was its roots in a theory of political obligation they regarded as premodern, antiliberal, and hence inhuman and irrational. Americans could well understand and celebrate soldiers like their own who bravely risked their lives in battle. But they could neither understand nor even begin to appreciate soldiers who seemed not to risk their lives because they did not regard their lives as their own to risk; Japanese soldiers seemed to prefer death to the dishonor that defeat would bring to their nation. Such behavior, as American commentators saw it, was not just another way of thinking about political obligation but rather its perversion, not another way of conceiving of human life but a repudiation of its fundamentals. "Japan," Price declared, "lacks respect for human life. We believe in living for our country. The Japanese believe in dying for their country."[31]

The thick particularism of Japanese nationalism contrasted sharply with not only American commitment to transnational liberal principles but also the private particularism that was integral to mobilizing

Americans for World War II. Japanese arguments for political obligation to an organic state struck Americans as either too particular (because nonliberal) or not particular enough (because too political).

This latter contrast is best illustrated by the differences between the familial ideology of the two nations. The Navy claimed that "the family, rather than the individual as in our country, is the basic unit in Japanese life," but this claim about the United States is countered by a considerable body of evidence to the contrary.[32] For example, the following lines from the memoir of a Japanese soldier reprinted in *Time* magazine might easily have been written by one of his American adversaries (a similarity *Time* implicitly acknowledged in offering the story as evidence that the Japanese soldier might after all be "human"): "A soldier offered me his shovel, I took it and unconsciously traced the characters Father and Mother in the soft sand. Then I erased them and wrote the names of my wife and children. I touched the good-luck omen my mother had given me and I thought of her prayers for my safety."[33] Americans no less than the Japanese conceived of the war as a war for the defense of the family. In their efforts to mobilize the nation, the American liberal state and its allies in Hollywood and the War Advertising Council appealed not only to the thin universalism of transcendent moral principles but also to the more concrete moral obligations of the private sphere, and no obligation ranked higher in American war propaganda than the obligation to protect the family.[34]

Yet fighting for the family meant two profoundly different things in the United States and Japan. Löwith explained the difference:

The Japanese family is not a family in our sense, i.e., a man, his wife, and their children, separated from the parents and grandparents. The Japanese family is not an individual unity but the center and substance of state and society, including parents and grandparents. The grandfather is the head of the family while the grandson is the guarantee of an un-interrupted ancestor cult. . . . The source and climax of the whole family and ancestral system is the Imperial family, which derives from the Sun Goddess. The "big house" (*Oyake*) of the Imperial family is the principal house from which descend all the "small houses" (*Koyake*) of the people. [National] loyalty and filial piety are in the same line and connected by the ancestor cult. Every Japanese child bows at the beginning of his classes in the direction of the Imperial palace in Tokyo just as he pays re-spect to the tablets of the family shrine. Fatherland and Imperial house are for the Japanese the same. Hence the social and moral foundations of the Japanese "patriotism" are very different from what we call patriot-ism, nationalism and imperialism.[35]

Thus, while Americans thought of themselves as a "state of families," an aggregate of idealized, bourgeois, nuclear families, the Japanese conceived of themselves as a "family state," an organic whole in which the nation was quite literally a single extended family. Political obliga-tion was "the extension of the filial piety to the Imperial family, sup-ported by tradition and emotional appeal."[36]

Americans saw in Japanese political culture an illegitimate expan-sion of the deepest and most abiding of private obligations. To some, the Japanese family state even made Japanese nationalism "much more substantial and total than that of the totalitarian states."[37] More than willing themselves to conceive of the state as an instrument for discharging private family obligations, Americans were baffled by a people that seemed unable (like good liberals) to draw a clear line be-tween private and public spheres or to distinguish the body politic from the family circle.

The Allure of Solidarity

There were few relativists in the foxholes of American commentary on Japanese political culture during World War II. The Japanese were not merely different; they were abominable. Their political culture not only had to be understood but also destroyed. On occasion, critics of Japanese political theory could give vent to a rhetoric of annihilation less common among those who regarded the Japanese as a neo-feudal historical sport than among those who saw them as an inferior race of monkeys or vermin. Japan, Willis Lamott argued, must be so thoroughly defeated that "the whole fabric of modern Japanese spiritual and ethical life would be torn to shreds." The only way to deal with Japan's dangerous philosophy would be to inflict "a defeat of such an overwhelming and disastrous nature as to reorient the nation and set it upon the task of building its life upon totally different bases." Given their "savage" way of thinking, Otto Tolischus argued, the Japanese must be subjected to "ideological extermination."[38]

Nonetheless, a certain grudging admiration for Japanese political culture and the solidarity it produced occasionally crept into American views of the enemy. *Fortune* may have been wholly ironic in bemoaning the fact that "submissiveness is a Japanese weapon that our war engineers cannot reproduce," but others were willing to lament without irony the superior ideological resources the Japanese had to hand. "The enemy has discovered a part of man that our materialists don't think about very much," Emmet Lavery observed, "the thing some of us call a soul. True, we appeal to it somewhat in our churches and in our schools. But does our spiritual dynamic move our people to the degree that the spiritual dynamic of the enemy has moved the Germans and the Japanese?" The Japanese had the advantage of "love of country plus a high pressure form of political mysticism." Even Tolischus saw the "savage code" of the Japanese as a two-edged sword; Japanese leaders had been able "to instill in their followers a faith which is fiendish enough to produce the foul deeds now being recorded but also strong enough to inspire the loyalty, the courage, the endurance, the toughness and fanaticism" with which the Japanese were fighting.[39]

Americans understood the need for solidarity in wartime and the special difficulties that an "individualistic" people like themselves had in sustaining such a collective spirit. They were not inclined in ordinary circumstances to think in terms of "We-All," but they knew it might not be a bad idea in the midst of a total war. Sometimes, they were even willing to entertain the notion of their nation as a single family, "one fighting family . . . 130,000,000 of us," as a General Electric advertisement put it. Representing the United States as a family state did, to be sure, prove extraordinarily difficult to do. It was impossible to do so photographically because, unlike the Japanese, Americans had no conventional rituals of family-state solidarity to offer the camera. At best, one could only paint pictures of the state of families and try to pass them off as something thicker. The GE ad, for example, featured six separate panels of six different families engaged in wartime production and conservation. And most activities depicted in the ad were organized by the market, an institution designed to produce collective goods in the absence of self-conscious collective solidarity. Other graphic representations suffered from the absence of any convincing American iconography of the family state. Portraits of a national family headed by Uncle Sam appeared occasionally, but a political theory rooted in avuncular authority was difficult to imagine, let alone represent. Nonetheless, such ventures in family-state thinking do suggest that Americans appreciated a thicker patriotism than that which liberalism afforded them.[40]

WE-ALL

The Japanese attack on the United States instantly changed our trend of thought in this country.

Before that attack some of us thought in terms of "I", others in terms of "we". Neither of those terms expresses our feelings today.

"I" represents only one person.

"We" may mean only two or a few persons.

Our slogan now is WE-ALL, which means every loyal individual in the United States.

We are facing a long, hard job, but when the United States decides to fight for a cause, it is in terms of WE-ALL, and nothing can or will stop us.

President Roosevelt, our Commander-in-Chief, can be certain that WE-ALL are back of him, determined to protect our country, our form of government, and the freedoms which we cherish.

President,
International Business Machines Corporation

IBM ventures an argument for solidarity and collective identity, *Time*, 17 January 1942. Reprinted by permission, International Business Machines Corporation.

An attraction to a thicker patriotism was evident as well in the persistence during the war of republican and ethnocultural notions of
American identity. Only rarely does one find vaguely neorepublican
representations of democratic citizenship that portray it as not merely
instrumental to protecting universal liberal ideals or to discharging
private moral obligations but as an end in itself and one constitut-
ing American identity.[41] Far more often, the Pacific war was conceived
as a race war, and propagandists appealed to white American solidarity against a yellow peril. Such appeals were difficult for representatives of the American state itself to make officially because they were
allied with the Chinese, anxious not to alienate African Americans,
and eager to distance themselves from Nazi racism. Nonetheless, government officials did employ an ethnocultural understanding of American citizenship to legitimate the internment of Japanese Americans.
Ironically, no Americans advanced a more lucid and consistent case
for a liberal understanding of American national identity than those
Japanese Americans who resisted the efforts of the American state to
deny them their rights on particularistic racial grounds.[42]

Yet whatever the attractions of a thicker patriotism and a more
genuinely political conception of their obligations to the war effort,
few Americans were willing to purchase enhanced solidarity at the ex-
pense of their own individual liberties. Whatever the defects of a thin,
liberal nationalism, they paled in the face of the oppression that the
thickly "collectivist" Japanese state visited upon its subjects. And thin
liberalism and thick authoritarianism seemed to most Americans the
only alternatives. One can imagine a thicker, yet nonetheless liberal,
American nationalism in which liberal ideals are conceived not as
transcendent, universal rights but as the values of a particular national polity, rooted not in human nature but in the particularities

and peculiarities of American history and culture.[43] But that would make the United States a nation among nations—and no longer nature's nation. This alternative was a possibility that few Americans were willing to entertain during World War II and one that remains difficult for many to swallow sixty years later.

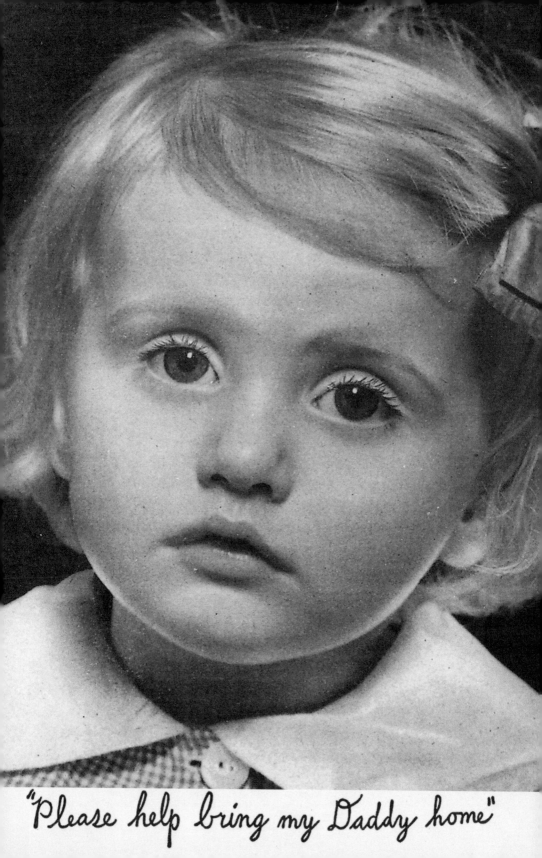

"Please help bring my Daddy home"

Fighting for the American Family

Private Commitments and Political Obligations

War, perhaps more so than any other experience, heightens reflection and debate about political obligation. During wartime, we are more inclined to ask ourselves why we are obliged not only to obey the laws of our state but why we (or our loved ones) are obliged to risk our lives to defend it. Once the question of "why we fight" becomes concrete, for some of us horribly concrete, we all take on the mantle of political philosopher.

For Americans, more often than not, this mantle is that of a *liberal* political philosopher. Hence, as we have already seen, we might reasonably expect that the popular political culture of a polity whose dominant public discourse is liberalism, such

Electric Auto-Lite advertisement, *Time*,
7 February 1944.

as the modern United States, would manifest the peculiarities of political obligation in the liberal tradition of political philosophy. Most notable among these peculiarities, is the difficulty that liberal theorists, elite and popular alike, have had in arguing that a war effort entails an obligation to work, fight, or die for one's country as a particular *political* community.

Some critical philosophers' contention that liberalism lacks a coherent conception of *political* obligation is, I have argued, reflected in American discourse during World War II. By and large, the American state and other propagandists relied then on arguments—such as those in the Atlantic Charter or Franklin Roosevelt's "Four Freedoms" speech—positing moral obligations that transcended those to a particular political community. We saw such arguments at work in the American notion that illiberal Japanese political culture was at odds with values that were not simply American but universal and human.

But even more interestingly, American propagandists also appealed to Americans both as individuals and as families to join the war effort so that they could discharge essentially private moral obligations, obligations that were not transnational but rather subnational. Moreover, the more elusive evidence of the felt obligations of Americans suggests that they found latter sort of appeals most compelling and that such appeals coincided most often with their own notions of "what we are fighting for."

In the discourse of obligation during World War II, no private obligation outranked the one to the family, and it is the place of the family in the prescriptions Americans were offered for "why we fight" that I will address in this chapter. But to better indicate the questions and hypotheses at stake, I should first say a bit more about the difficulties that liberalism and the liberal state have with political obligation.

Liberal Obligations

It is fair to say that the liberal theory of political obligation is in deep trouble these days. Arguing from a variety of perspectives, several contemporary philosophers have examined the basis for political obligation offered by the liberal tradition's philosophical giants from Thomas Hobbes to John Rawls and have concluded that, as Carole Pateman puts it, "political obligation in the liberal democratic state constitutes an insoluble problem; insoluble because political obligation cannot be given expression within the context of liberal democratic institutions."[1]

This critique of the liberal theory of political obligation has advanced on at least two fronts. On the one hand, such philosophers as John Simmons have used the tools of analytic philosophy to demonstrate that such traditional foundations for the liberal theory of political obligation as the tacit consent of citizens to the authority of the state or the reciprocal exchange of benefits between citizens and the state cannot provide an adequate account of or justification for obligation. On the other hand, such communitarian critics of liberalism as Michael Walzer have slighted these difficulties in favor of raising doubts about whether the liberal theory is a coherent an account of political obligation—that is, of obligations that men and women have as citizens. It is this latter critique that is most pertinent to my discussion of familial obligations and interests in the thinking of Americans about their commitment to the war effort during World War II.[2]

In an essay titled "The Obligation to Die for the State," Walzer addresses the problem of obligation in the context of war and asks whether the obligation citizens have to the state can be made the motive for risking their lives. The answer to this question, he suggests, depends in critical respects on the nature of the state, and, in the case of the liberal state, the answer is no. The reason for this, he argues, is that the purpose of the liberal state, as conceived in the social contract tradition of Hobbes, Locke, and their successors, is to secure the lives of the individuals who form it, and, consequently, "a man who dies for the state defeats his only purpose in forming the state: death is the contradiction of politics. A man who risks his life for the state accepts the insecurity which it was the only end of his political obedience to avoid: war is the failure of politics. Hence there can be no political obligation either to die or to fight."[3]

When a war begins, political authorities in a liberal society may, as Hobbes put it, invite their subjects to "protect their protection," but in doing so they admit that they have failed to hold up their end of the bargain on which the state rests. Peculiar in any case as a call to men and women to risk their lives for their instrument, the invitation is doubly peculiar as one to defend an instrument that has failed its function. As Walzer says, when individuals "protect their protection they are doing nothing more than defending themselves, and so they cannot protect their protection after their protection ceases to protect them. At that point, it ceases to be their protection. The state has no value over and above the value of the lives of the concrete individuals whose safety it provides. No man has a common life to defend, but only an individual life." The liberal state at war is like a bodyguard hired to protect the lives and property of a family, who then gets into a fight with a gang threatening that family and turns to his clients and asks them to protect him. They have no obligation to do so since they hired the bodyguard precisely to avoid this situation. If they fight the gang, they do so because of obligations they have to protect themselves and one another, not out of any political obligation to the bodyguard-state.[4]

Walzer links this difficulty liberalism has with political obligation to its atomistic individualism and its largely negative view of liberty, which create a citizen who is an individual protected by the state from interference by other individuals or by the state itself. The liberal position suggests "an indefinite number of distinct and singular relations between the individual citizens and the authorities as a body—a pattern that might best be symbolized by a series of vertical lines. There are no horizontal connections among citizens as citizens." The state is thought of "as an instrument which serves individual men (or families) but not or not necessarily as an instrument wielded by these men themselves" as constituents of a political community. Walzer concludes that any theory like liberalism which "begins with the absolute independence of freely willing individuals and goes on to treat politics and the state as instrumental to the achievement of individual purposes would seem by its very nature incapable of describing ultimate obligation."[5]

It is important to add, as Walzer does, that this difficulty in liberal theory does not mean that citizens will not go to war and fight and die on behalf of ethical, if not political, obligations. As he says:

> Moved by love, sympathy, or friendship, men in liberal society can and obviously do incur ultimate obligations. They may even find themselves in situations where they are or think they are obliged to defend the state which defends in turn the property and enjoyment of their friends and families. But if they then actually risk their lives or die, they do so because they have incurred private obligations which have nothing to do with politics. The state may shape the environment within which these obligations are freely incurred, and it may provide the occasions and the means for their fulfillment. But this is only to say that, when states make war and men fight, the reasons of the two often are and ought to be profoundly different.[6]

The fact that an argument is a bad one does not mean that it will not be made, and during World War II the American state did occasionally call upon its citizens to protect their protection, as if this amounted to something more than a plea to protect themselves. Less often, it "poached" on other nonliberal traditions, searching for more persuasive grounds for political obligation. More frequently, it invoked commitments to such abstract, universal values as "freedom" that Americans shared with others not as citizens but as fellow human beings. Yet what is most striking about propaganda for the "Good War"—as if tacitly acknowledging that these abstract, universal values were not compelling arguments for political obligation in a liberal society chastened by an earlier war's failure to make the world safe for democracy—is the degree to which proponents openly attempted, as Walzer's arguments suggest they might, to exploit private obligations to convince Americans to serve the cause of national defense. Such obligations—to families, to children, to parents, to friends, and generally, to an "American Way of Life" defined as a rich (and richly commodified) private realm of experience—were tirelessly invoked in the campaign to mobilize Americans for World War II, and they formed the centerpiece of the propaganda produced by the state and its allies in Hollywood, the War Advertising Council, and elsewhere.

Norman Rockwell's War

Students of popular political theory will often find it in some unusual places, and I would like to begin my discussion of the mobilization of familial obligations in World War II with a story about the work of an American not usually numbered among the nation's great political philosophers: Norman Rockwell.

Sometime in 1942 Rockwell and his friend, neighbor, and fellow illustrator, Mead Schaeffer, decided to contribute to the war effort by offering their services as painters to the American government, but they were delayed initially because Rockwell could not come up with any ideas for posters that he really liked. "I wanted to do something bigger than a war poster," he wrote in his autobiography, "make some statement about why the country was fighting the war."[7]

Rockwell thought the idea he was looking for might be found in Franklin Roosevelt's proclamation of the "four essential human freedoms"—freedom of speech, freedom of worship, freedom from want, and freedom from fear—that Americans hoped to secure abroad, but he was deterred by Roosevelt's language which he found "so noble, platitudinous really, that it stuck in my throat." "No, I said to myself, it doesn't go, how am I to illustrate that? I'm not noble enough. Besides, nobody I know is reading the proclamation either, in spite of the fanfare and hullabaloo about it in the press and on the radio." One night, while tossing and turning in bed with this problem, the solution struck him:

I suddenly remembered how Jim Edgerton had stood up in town meeting and said something that everybody else disagreed with. But they had let him have his say. No one shouted him down. My gosh, I thought, that's it. There it is. Freedom of Speech. I'll illustrate the Four Freedoms using my Vermont neighbors as models. I'll express the ideas in simple, everyday scenes. Freedom of Speech—a New England town meeting. Freedom from Want—a Thanksgiving dinner. Take them out of the noble language of the proclamation and put them in terms everybody can understand.[8]

Rockwell and Schaeffer then set out for Washington armed with rough sketches of their ideas, but they met with little success. The Office of War Information, one administrator told them, intended to use only the work of "real artists."

On the way back to Vermont, a discouraged Rockwell stopped off in Philadelphia to meet with Ben Hibbs, the editor of the *Saturday Evening Post*, and happened to show him his sketches for *The Four Freedoms*. Hibbs found the sketches very exciting, pledged to publish them in the *Post*, and urged Rockwell to drop everything else he was doing. Early in 1943 the illustrations were published in four consecutive issues of the magazine.

The illustrations elicited an enormous response. Requests to reprint them poured into the *Post* offices, including many from government agencies that now found a use for them. Millions of reprints were made, and they were distributed all over the world. Subsequently, the Treasury Department used the original paintings as part of a war-bond tour that garnered nearly $133 million in bonds. "Those four pictures," Hibbs wrote, "quickly became the best known and most appreciated paintings of that era. They appeared right at a time when the war was going against us on the battle fronts, and the American people needed the inspirational message which they conveyed so forcefully and so beautifully."[9]

What was the message that these pictures conveyed so forcefully and beautifully? It was, with one notable exception (to which I shall return), that Americans were fighting World War II to discharge essentially private obligations. And two of the four paintings conveyed the message that the people of the United States were fighting for the family.

Freedom from Fear was the only one of the four paintings that referred directly to the war. In this painting a concerned mother and father look in on their sleeping children. Their concerns on this occasion are, however, extraordinary (perhaps indicated by the fact that

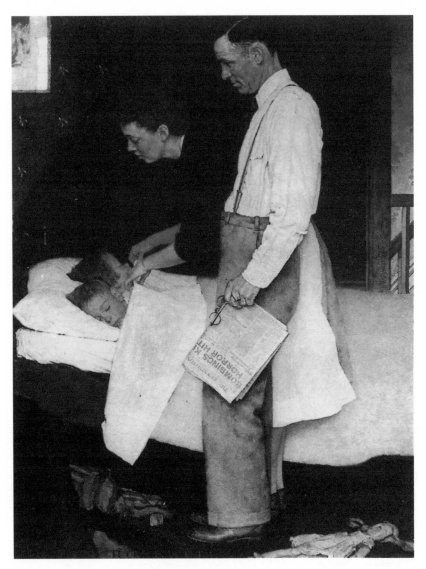

Norman Rockwell, *Freedom from Fear*, 1943.

both are in the children's room simultaneously), for they have been reading about the bombing of London in the newspaper that the father holds in his hand. As Rockwell said, the painting is supposed to say, "Thank God we can put our children to bed with a feeling of security, knowing they will not be killed in the night." The threat of bombing conveyed in the illustration, as Stephen Vincent Benet said in the essay accompanying it in the *Post*, is a threat that the geographical isolation of the United States cannot withstand, and hence children must rely on the courage of their parents to protect them from death and the fear of death. Freedom from fear, Benet intoned, "goes to the roots of life—to a man and a woman and their children and the home they can make and keep."[10]

Familial interests and obligations were also central to Rockwell's vision of *Freedom from Want*. This painting portrayed a Thanksgiving dinner for which an extended family has gathered (and to which the viewer is invited). This image was intended to convey the message that Americans are fighting to protect the opportunities they had, as Americans, to provide for their own and their families' material needs. In this painting, Roosevelt's most controversial "freedom" was rendered not, as Vice President Henry Wallace would have had it, as the foundation of a global New Deal that guaranteed every child a quart of milk a day, but rather as the defense of the familial surfeit during a peculiarly American holiday.[11]

The Home Front

Rockwell's translation of Roosevelt's noble, platitudinous, abstract, and universalist moral language into a more concrete, particular moral language centering on private obligations and commitments was far from idiosyncratic. Indeed, I would maintain that this translation is one of the most significant features of American propaganda during

Norman Rockwell, *Freedom from Want*, 1943.

World War II. Again and again, propagandists explicitly or implicitly contended, as an advertisement for US Rubber put it, that "words like *freedom* or *liberty* draw close to us only when we break them down into the *homely fragments of daily life*." And, more often than not, those fragments were literally "homely," that is, familial.[12]

Like Norman Rockwell, the American state and private corporations interpreted the obligations of Americans to support the war effort as a duty they owed to the family that raised them, the family they were themselves raising, the family they would someday raise, and/or, somewhat more abstractly, to the family as a social institution. The war, one ad said, was "this fight to keep our country a safe place for the wives we love, a place where our children can grow up free and unafraid," and no obligation ranked higher in American war propaganda than the obligation to protect the family.[13]

The enemy was repeatedly portrayed in posters and ads as a threat to the family, particularly its weaker members. The state, in turn, was shown in good liberal fashion as the protector of the family. In one very illuminating example of this argument, we find the Axis powers portrayed as Halloween vandals on a rampage. They have burned a family farm, an essentially private icon tied to "our Democratic institutions." Behind a tree Uncle Sam (literally "Uncle" Sam)—the American state—waits to foil their further mischief, armed with the rifle of American industrial might. In ads such as this, private corporations like Philco announced their eagerness to be a part of the family's arsenal, emphasizing that the sacrifices made in converting to war production would, as another ad put it, "help Daddy lick" the enemy.[14]

The Philco ad is interesting not only because it clearly indicates that Americans were fighting for home and family when they defended democratic institutions. It also provides a nice example of how the liberal state could represent itself as a family relative, "Uncle Sam,"

Fighting for the security of the family. Community Silverplate advertisement, *Life*, 19 October 1942.

"Are they coming over here to fight, daddy?"

NO, Sister, they're not coming over here — not if all the power of American ships and planes, and all the sacrifice of American men can stop them.

But they may try.

If they try, some may get through, for it is a wide sky, and bombs may crash here as they crashed on far-away Hawaii and in the distant Philippines.

Or even if they don't try, the work of enemies within our own gates may bring fires, explosions, damage to our busy defense plants.

So we must be ready—just in case.

Ready with quick help for the hurt and the suffering. Ready with merciful aid that is still great in America's heart, even in a world where such things as mercy and decency seem no longer to exist.

That's the job of the Red Cross — to dispense that merciful care and help wherever and whenever pain and suffering exist.

It's a big job, that will call for every effort the hundreds of thousands of Red Cross workers — nurses, disaster fighters and volunteer helpers — can put forth.

It will call for vast stores of medicines and supplies, food and clothing, bandages and equipment.

It will demand every penny of the fifty million dollars the Red Cross is now asking for, and more.

So every bit helps, Sister.

Every dollar your Daddy can bring up from the bottom of his pocket, every penny any man or woman can add to the check he or she writes now for the Red Cross.

The brave men awing, afloat and afield who take care of us sometimes need care too, and we must give it.

We give it when we give to the Red Cross, whether it be a little or a lot.

Send contributions to your local chapter

American Red Cross War Fund Campaign

Give and give generously — to your local chapter — to volunteer solicitors. Give when you can, where you can, as much as you can.

This page contributed to the American Red Cross by the publishers

Mobilizing Daddy. American Red Cross advertisement, *Life*, 19 January 1942.

"He won't let them hurt us ...will he, mommy?"

YOUNG flying officer...civilian air-raid warden...both enlisted to make America safe. He fights...she serves ...and both must be kept well and strong.

Illness, contagion must not be permitted to slacken our speed —or weaken the staggering blow our nation has set itself to deliver. Common colds, influenza, trench mouth and the like must not black out the work of thousands of willing hands. And health officials everywhere tell us that these illnesses are most commonly spread by indirect mouth-to-mouth contact at the common drinking place.

It is not surprising then that you meet Dixie Cups so frequently at soda fountains these days, at milk bars, at Army canteens, aboard our Naval ships...wherever thirst is quenched in public. Used but once and thrown away, these fresh clean paper cups break the chain of contagion.

DIXIE CUPS

DIXIE-VORTEX COMPANY, EASTON, PA., CHICAGO, ILL., TORONTO, CAN.

DIXIE CUPS are safeguards of health at all times ...everywhere. In the office, in the shop, in public places, at soda fountains, on trains

and airplanes, the common drinking vessel is a thing of the past. The expanding uses of Dixie Cups are but an indication of the trend of the times.

Putting a face to the protective state. Dixie Cup advertisement, *Life*, 16 March 1942.

Our Way to Handle Vandals!

THE Army-Navy "E" flags that fly above the Philco plants at Philadelphia, Trenton and Sandusky are citations of *Excellence* in the production of war equipment from our fighting forces to the men and women of Philco. They are symbols of the vital partnership between our soldiers of the front and our soldiers of production.

More than that, they are *battle flags* for America at home, symbols of the devotion and sacrifice beyond the line of duty which are the price of Victory. For that is the spirit in which industrial America, as the

War Department citation reads, is "accomplishing today what yesterday seemed impossible."

The Philco laboratories, machines and assembly lines are producing communications equipment, radios for tanks and airplanes, artillery fuzes and shells, electric storage batteries for the Army, Navy and War Production plants. They are doing their share to the end that America's might may strike the decisive blow for Victory. And that mankind may enjoy in freedom the more abundant life which will arise from the scientific miracles born of war.

This cartoon by Herbert Johnson is another in the series being drawn for Philco by America's leading editorial cartoonists to interpret the spirit of Philco's soldiers of production. It is being posted on bulletin boards of the Philco factories as a symbol to the men and women of Philco of the purpose and significance of their work in the united effort for Victory.

Free Limited Offer . . . While available, a full size reproduction of the original drawing by Herbert Johnson will be furnished gladly upon request. Simply address Philco Corporation, Philadelphia, Penna., and ask for Cartoon Number 27D.

PHILCO CORPORATION

America is conserving its resources for Victory. As you save on sugar, rubber, gasoline and all products of peace-time consumption, remember too to preserve the use of the things you own. Through its national service organizations, Philco offers, at reasonable and uniform charges, the means of prolonging the life of Philco products.

RADIOS, PHONOGRAPHS, REFRIGERATORS, AIR CONDITIONERS, RADIO TUBES ★ ★ INDUSTRIAL STORAGE BATTERIES FOR MOTIVE POWER, SIGNAL SYSTEMS, CONTROL AND AUXILIARY POWER

The liberal state as brave uncle. Philco Corporation advertisement, *Life*, 2 November 1942.

to obscure the fact that a declaration of war meant that it had failed to hold up the bargain struck with its citizens to protect them from death in exchange for their obedience. It was not Uncle Sam that was protecting the family during the war but fathers, mothers, and other relatives who went to war to keep Hitler, Mussolini, and Tojo from the door, and it was their private obligation to do so that the American state mobilized. Thus, to be true to the character of obligation in World War II, one would have to say that Uncle Sam, as depicted in this ad, represents not the American state but the host of real Uncle Sams organized by the state to fight for their families. The gun he wields represents the others, "our soldiers of production," who protected their homes by working in war plants.

Americans were instructed that they might discharge their obligation to protect home and family in a number of ways. Soldiers, of course, were called upon to risk their lives in combat for their loved ones, and their mothers—who, according to *Life*, stood for "home, love, faith, all the things they are fighting for"—were presented with blue stars to signify this commitment and gold stars to signify that their sons had made the ultimate sacrifice. Hollywood portrayed soldiers fighting for mothers, children, brides, and brides-to-be back home. For example, in the most poignant scene in one of the best combat films, *Guadalcanal Diary* (1943), a marine captain lying fatally wounded on the beach reaches in death for his helmet and the photograph of his family tucked in its webbing. For those who had no personal pin-ups of wives or girlfriends to plaster to the machines of war, the studios in cooperation with the state provided surrogates like Betty Grable. Far and away the most popular pin-up of the war, Grable was, as we will see, offered to soldiers less as an exotic sex goddess than as a symbol of the woman for whom American men were fighting.[15]

On the home front, civilians were urged to aid their soldier-protectors in the war for the family by working in defense plants, supporting the Red Cross, conserving vital materials, and buying war bonds. One life insurance company warned that men deferred in 1942 because they were fathers should be aware that "upon victory rests everything that means most to you as a father . . . the security of your home the safety and freedom of your children . . . the very *way of life* that America stands for" and recommended that these men supplement the protection victory afforded with the added fortification of a new insurance policy. Women who worked in factories to provide their protectors with the weapons they needed were assured that they were "fighting for freedom and all that means to women everywhere. You're fighting for a little house of your own, and a husband to meet every night at the door. You're fighting for the right to bring up your children without the shadow of fear."[16]

Some corporations argued that the war was not only being waged to protect the family but was also a blessing in disguise that would actually enhance family welfare. Restraints on consumer spending coupled with high wages and savings invested in war bonds had enabled consumers to engage in "installment buying in reverse" that would provide them with the home of their dreams after the war. "After the war," Revere Copper declared, "youth has a new world to look forward to. For today's young men and women can plan instead of dream, can be sure that the homes their parents merely wished for can become a reality for them. . . . In this war, we are fighting not only against our enemies, but for a better way of life for many more of us." The homes pictured in its ad were an example of what American families could have "by fighting, and sacrificing, and winning."

A few companies like furniture manufacturers W&J Sloane urged consumers not to wait for war's end to begin living this dream but to invest immediately in at least one major purchase that "can mean

Beyond the war waits happiness

After the war youth has a new world to look forward to. For today's young men and women can plan instead of dream, can be sure that the homes their parents merely wished for can become a reality for them.

Here is such a home where every window can frame a garden view, where there is space for all the pleasures and purposes of living, where doors can move aside to enlarge favorite rooms or to include garden and terrace as part of the living area.

Here is more than shelter from the weather, and more than simple provision for physical comfort. This house is designed to surround you with the things that lift your heart and make you glad.

It is a house to be lived in for a lifetime. If your family grows so that more rooms are needed, you can add them. They have already been provided for in the original plan. Even the closet and storage space have been carefully worked out to hold the many possessions which all families accumulate through the years.

Complete with the new inventions and conveniences which copper has brought to modern living, such a house can be made available, through mass production, for not more than $2,000. And the 36 parts of which it is built can be assembled in diver-

sified arrangements, so it never need look or be just like your neighbor's. For you and those you cherish, it can always be—Home.

A. LAWRENCE KOCHER

In this war, we are fighting not only against our enemies, but *for a better* way of life for many more of us. Homes such as those Mr. Kocher has designed are an example of what we can have by fighting and sacrificing, and *winning*.

Great architects and engineers have developed brilliant plans for homes after the war. New techniques will be available for building them at lower cost: Enduring, rust-proof copper will be waiting to give them protection against weather and termites, to help heat them more economically, to insure rust-free water, to afford new comforts and conveniences — to make your home of tomorrow better to own, or rent, or sell.

All of us today are working for Uncle Sam. There is no copper for building, or for any other purpose except winning the war. But in Revere's laboratories, research is continually pressing forward in preparation for the better, happier living that victory can bring us all.

Floor plan showing one of the many attractive arrangements possible with this house.

Naturally, in this limited space, Mr. Kocher could give you only a bare outline of his conception. Revere has prepared an illustrated booklet with complete details. We will gladly send it to you, free. Write us.

REVERE
COPPER AND BRASS INCORPORATED
Executive Offices: 230 Park Avenue, New York

Defending and extending the "American Way of Life," *Life*, 20 July 1942.

home . . . the root, the core, the propulsion of our lives." The better way of life, the "American Way of Life" that these ads and other propaganda described, had little to do with citizenship. It was above all a rewarding domestic life for which Americans were fighting—a private sphere filled with goods and services provided by those who had halted production so that their customers might effectively defend homes that in the wake of victory would be even more densely cluttered with commodities.[17]

I could easily provide many examples of documents that argue that "we fight for the family." Such prescriptive evidence may not directly represent the obligations that Americans felt during the war. But it is fair to say that American propagandists—especially those working for private corporations—appealed to attitudes and convictions they believed (or their research told them) were widespread in their audiences. Moreover, the popularity of Rockwell's paintings suggests that he struck a nerve as well. And what evidence we have of the felt obligations of Americans (principally soldiers) suggests that an adman did not fabricate the claim that Americans were fighting for the family.[18]

Nonliberal Obligations

If the only theory Americans lived in World War II was liberalism and if they only thought about their obligations to the war effort in liberal, nonpolitical terms, the story would be neat and probably wrong. Historians no longer contend that liberalism is the only American political tradition, even if few doubt its hegemony. Though I am less disposed than some to stress the persistence in the United States of an adversarial republican ideology, one can now and again hear its faint echoes in World War II. Moreover, theory—especially lived theory— is rarely consistent. We shore up the weak flanks of our thinking with arguments to which our most cherished premises may not entitle us, preferring a jerry-built structure of thought that covers all the bases to a logical masterpiece that leaves us without the benefits that logic would deny. I would like to conclude then with a look at two documents that reflect nonliberal perspectives that occasionally crept into the discourse about obligation during the war.

A 1942 Birds Eye Foods advertisement attempts a nonliberal argument that interprets "fighting for the family" in a way quite different from the liberal one I have discussed. Occasionally, to borrow some terms from political philosopher Amy Gutmann, Americans tried to think of themselves during the war not as a "state of families" but as a "family state" or, as a General Electric ad put it, "just one fighting family . . . 130,000,000 of us!" In the Birds Eye ad, which contrasts with Rockwell's later use of the Thanksgiving theme, the nation is portrayed as a family sitting down to Thanksgiving dinner at a table headed by Uncle Sam. Expressions such as this, it seems to me, grew out of anxieties about the capacity of a nation of "individualists" or even individual families to achieve the level of cooperation and solidarity necessary to win the war. If the nation was to win, the ad suggests, its citizens must think of themselves as members of a single family, bound together by affective ties akin to those they shared with their closest relatives.[19]

Yet this argument was rare because it presented a grave difficulty: It came perilously close to the theories of political obligation advanced by the enemy, particularly the Japanese, who justified dying for the state (the emperor) on the grounds that theirs was (quite literally) a family state. As we have seen, Americans widely attacked this theory, and some perceived it as evidence that the Japanese were a subhuman race. Americans were urged, in effect, to see themselves as defending liberalism and its thin conception of citizenship from the evil of a

Your Government *urges* you, please, to eat WELL and HEARTILY!

AMERICA, THERE'S A WAR ON!

A war for our survival as a free country. A war whose winning will take *greater* efforts than we ever dreamed possible. Heroic efforts and sacrifices from our fighting men. Grim, endless toil from the men and women who back them up on production lines.

To supply the energy for this daily battle, you need more than *well* and *heart*. You need FOOD. *Lots of it.* And your Government, through the National Nutrition Advisory Committee, urges you—in these hurried days —*not* to get in the habit of the "gulp-and-run" meal.

Get food that *looks* good . . . *tastes* good. Nourishing food that gives your body the *vital elements* it must have for sustained drive!

On the list of such foods are Birds Eye Frosted Foods. They are *appetizing* . . . *delicious* . . . *nutritious.* Appetizing, because they are painstakingly selected for quality. Deli-cious, because they are *ocean-fresh* or *farm-fresh*—quick-frozen at their *peak of goodness!* For this same reason, Birds Eye Foods are *naturally rich* in healthful vitamins and food values.

With Birds Eye Foods, there is little, if any, *loss* of important food values through exposure to air, or en route to markets. Instead —and we must repeat this—they are *quick frozen* and *held for you* at zero temperature. This captures not only flavor and freshness, but vital vitamins and minerals which your body needs!

EAT—and *eat well!* There are over 60 varieties of Birds Eye Frosted Foods—Meats, Seafood, Poultry, Fruits, and Vegetables.

Straining to represent a family state. Birds Eye Frosted Foods advertisement, *Life*, 29 June 1942.

nation wedded to a much thicker and thereby oppressive conception of citizenship and political obligation. Yet a note of grudging admiration for the family state sometimes snuck into these denunciations, and it is evident in the Birds Eye ad.[20]

Perhaps what the ad suggests best is the difficulty of coherently reconciling stronger theories of political obligation with liberal premises. Representing the American state as an uncle and not a father (or mother) made the family state difficult to depict because such avuncular authority was not easy to define. On the other hand, placing Uncle Sam rather than a father-surrogate at the head of the table deflected comparisons with the ideology of the enemy. Had the artist put the carving knife in the hands of, say, FDR, howls of protest against creeping dictatorship would have gone up from the precincts of the Republican party if not elsewhere. Hence, this ad stands as a statement less of collective than of aggregate purpose and, at most, a description of wished-for social rather than political bonds.

Nonliberal theories of political obligation need not be undemocratic, and sometimes during the war Americans were offered a glimpse of this alternative. Perhaps the best example of such a democratic theory was *Freedom of Speech*, the exceptional painting in Rockwell's series on FDR's "four freedoms."[21] It is the only picture of the four to portray a public scene, and it envisions a political community and a democratic, participatory, deliberative politics. It would not be stretching too far, I think, to say that the painting celebrates the public life and speech akin to that later eulogized by Hannah Arendt: "a way of life in which speech and only speech made sense and where the central concern of all citizens was to talk with each other."[22] Yet, unlike Arendt, Rockwell imagined the polis as a socially egalitarian community in which a working-class man (modeled on a filling-station attendant) speaks as an equal among men with white collars and in which even women are allowed to participate. He thus paints a moment in the politics of a state that some democratic philosophers have contrasted to the liberal state, not as a bodyguard or an insurance company for the private interests of citizens but a political community providing a common life for citizens as citizens.

Rockwell's portrait of this political community was, I think, unwitting. As the anecdote about the origins of *The Four Freedoms* indicates, what impressed him about this meeting was the fact that Jim Edgerton was allowed to voice his objections on a proposed policy without being shouted down by his neighbors. It was not political community that Rockwell saw himself celebrating in his painting, but tolerance of individual dissent, the use of free speech to protect private conscience from the state. This is the meaning Booth Tarkington gave to free speech in his accompanying essay, a fable about a meeting between Hitler and Mussolini in the Alps in 1912 in which each plots to become dictator of his respective country by destroying free speech. The painting eluded Rockwell's intentions, however, principally because he happened to live in a part of the country where a remnant of face-to-face participatory democracy survived, and he placed his dissenter (who is difficult to recognize as such) in the midst of this remnant.[23]

Citizens would be obliged to die for such a participatory democracy to protect the common life they share, so such a state could lay claim to political obligations. Walzer finds this conception of the state in Rousseau's republican version of the social contract, where individuals undergo a qualitative transformation in moving from nature into civil society, a move that makes all the difference. In Rousseau's state the citizen receives from his active participation in a political community "a second life, a moral life, which is not his sole possession, but whose reality depends upon the continued existence of his fellow-

Nonliberal, republican democracy. Norman Rockwell, *Freedom of Speech*, 1943.

citizens and of their association." From this perspective, according to Walzer,

> a good society is one in which the new man, a moral member of a moral body, achieves his fullest development. The very instincts of pre-social man are overwhelmed and above all the instinct for self-preservation. When the state is in danger, its citizens rush to its defense, forgetful of all personal danger. They die willingly for the sake of the state because the state is their common life. So long as the state survives, something of the citizen lives on, even after the natural man is dead. The state, or rather the common life of the citizens, generates those "moral goods" for which, according to Rousseau, men can in fact be obligated to die.[24]

This is obviously a quite different conception of the state and of citizenship than the one I have been discussing, one in which the citizen has "the lively sense of oneself as a participant in a free state, concerned for the common good" rather than "a lively longing for private pleasure." Walzer is obviously attracted to this nonliberal alternative, though he admits that it makes for a "hard politics" and is an ideal that "fails to describe any reality we know or can project for the future." Moreover, one cannot completely discount the worries that liberal critics have expressed about the harmonies one finds between Rousseau's descriptions of this hard democratic politics and the organic ideologies legitimating the even harder politics of authoritarian states. For my purposes, what is most important is Walzer's contention that this democratic ideal inheres in the feeling of some Americans that citizenship must amount to more than liberalism allows and in the sense of these citizens (now a bare majority of registered voters) that they should continue to participate in the minimal public life that the liberal state has conceded to democracy. Important as well is his suggestion that this participatory ideal functions ideologically in the liberal state to counteract the absence in the liberal theory of obligation to a "horizontal" political community. "This imposing and difficult ideal," he notes, "becomes an ideology whenever we are told that we are already citizens, men at or near our very best, and that our country is a nation of citizens." This is "mystification of the worst sort," yet it serves a useful purpose in that it keeps the ideal alive: "Ideology is the social element within which ideals survive."[25]

Freedom of Speech was Rockwell's favorite painting in the series and much of his audience's favorite as well, maybe because it conceived of obligation as communitarian and thoroughly political and provided an attractive alternative to the liberal conception of obligation as private and apolitical, calling for citizens to fight for the family and other private commitments, though these obligations were no less moral than those represented in the portrait of the town meeting. This painting was also the most thoroughly ideological in the series because it portrayed the hard politics of a nonliberal, democratic state unavailable to most yet appealing to many Americans; the painting contended that this was their politics and asked that they risk their lives for it. Yet *Freedom of Speech* also served to keep alive the ideal it represented. And those who remain wedded to this difficult and distant ideal may take some comfort in its appearance in a Norman Rockwell painting, which would guarantee, one would think, that it not be dismissed as un-American simply because it is not liberal.

"I Want a Girl, Just Like the Girl That Married Harry James"

American Women and the Problem of Political Obligation

As the 1988 presidential election campaign wound down to its conclusion, a reporter from the *New York Times* made a valiant effort to elicit the candidates' opinions on "the subject of culture." Perhaps unduly worried about Southern votes, George H. W. Bush went on at length about his fondness for country music and *Bassmaster* magazine. He also revealed that, when he was a young navy pilot during World War II, he had named four of his planes "Barbara" after his girlfriend, but he denied that he had gone in for pin-ups of Betty Grable or Rita Hayworth. "I didn't pin 'em up because I was, like, engaged to Barbara Bush. . . . Those pin-ups were all over our ship, but I'd like to plead innocent myself." Bush did, however, confess

Betty Grable and Harry James celebrate their wedding in Las Vegas, 1945.

that he had "glanced" at the pin-ups of his shipmates, and that when he glanced, he said, he liked Doris Day best.[1]

What follows suggests that Bush need not have been so sheepish on the subject of pin-ups. The sailors who pinned up Rita Hayworth were engaged in a common activity with those, like the president, who named their planes after their fiancées. Though Barbara Bush may not have been "just like the girl that married Harry James," she and Betty Grable were part of the same story.

That tale is part of the wider story I have told in the previous two chapters, for my interest in pin-ups is not what one might expect. I started thinking about pin-ups during a study of how Americans conceived of political obligation during World War II. This study, as we have seen, is an effort to see whether the political culture of a liberal polity such as the United States reflects empirically the claim that liberal theory lacks a coherent conception of political obligation, as a number of political philosophers have concluded (and whose conclusion I find persuasive). My aim is to identify the philosophy of obligation at work in American practices and institutions and to highlight its distinctive features by studying a moment when Americans had reason to be more explicit than usual about such matters.

Again, consistent with the expectations derived from political theory, I contend that, with some exceptions, Americans during World War II were not called upon, strictly speaking, to conceive of their obligation to participate in the war effort as a *political* obligation to work, fight, or die for their country. By and large, the representatives of the state and other American propagandists relied on two different moral arguments, neither of which constituted a claim of political obligation. First, they appealed to putatively universal moral values transcending obligations to the United States as a particular political community. Second, they implored Americans as individuals and as families to join the war effort to help protect the state that protected them—an appeal, philosophers have argued, characteristic of liberal states and one that, at bottom, is an appeal to go to war to discharge *private* obligations. Over the course of the war, this latter prescription became increasingly prominent, and the more elusive evidence of the felt obligations of Americans suggests that they found this appeal most compelling and that it coincided most often with their own notions of "what we are fighting for."[2]

Another important body of evidence supporting this hypothesis is what might be termed the cultural construction of women as objects of obligation. I want to analyze that process in this chapter, examining principally how communication elites fabricated women as icons of male obligation. I also will suggest how women functioned as such for soldiers and how women themselves participated in their mobilization as a private interest for which men would fight. I will focus on the pin-up, one of the most prominent documents in World War II material culture, and, in particular, on the image of the most popular movie star to appear on the walls of barracks from the Aleutians to North Africa: Betty Grable.[3]

Pin-Ups as Moral Arguments

Three years before the United States entered the war, a team of copywriters drew up a recruiting advertisement to show what wartime enlistment propaganda might look like. Though the most apparent feature of this ad is its racism—its call to white Americans to prevent "yellow feet" from ever reaching American soil—this document also anticipates the privatization of obligation in World War II propaganda. It urges men to enlist so that they might discharge a private obligation (the "'other fellow' won't stop them") to the women they, as individuals, protect ("your sister, your wife, your sweetheart"). The

appeal distinguishes this ad from other instances of Allied "rape propaganda," of which it is a part. Often such propaganda portrays women
simply as the booty of war and appeals to men to protect their property in women's bodies from enemy male competitors.[4] The "Your Sister" ad, however, represents a more complex bond of obligation tying
American men to the women of their society. The copy suggests that
the rights American men claim to "their" women's bodies are linked to
a set of corresponding obligations: The "yellow hand of lust" threatens
not so much to expropriate the bounty of the soldiers' own lust as it
does to rupture a moral relationship between them and the women
in their lives. It also indicates that this relationship extends to their
sisters—and to other women to whom they have no proprietary sexual claim. When American soldiers said, as they often did, that they
were "fighting for" American women, they were sometimes identifying
women as the spoils of war, but more often "for" meant "for whom" or
"on behalf of." They were articulating the moral obligations of the
"protector" to the "protected," a relationship ethically problematic in
its own right but nonetheless different from that of a man to a woman
viewed simply as sexual property.

A similar argument is implicit in one of the ubiquitous visual
components of the war's cultural landscape: the pin-up. Unlike the
"naughty postcard" that American troops brought back from France
during World War I, the pin-up circulated above ground in World
War II, and the Hollywood pin-up did so with official sanction. Despite the concerns of religious groups and some officials about the
immorality of pin-ups, the United States government and the film industry cooperated closely during the war in producing and distribut-
ing millions of photographs of Hollywood's leading ladies and rising
starlets, and these pictures decorated the walls of barracks, the bulk-
heads of ships, and the fuselages of planes on all fronts. I suspect that

That this shall not be
<u>Your</u> Sister!

Will a yellow hand of lust fall roughly on the white shoulder of *your* sister?

"Not while I've an ounce of manhood in my soul or a drop of blood in my body!" Naturally, that's your answer. BUT . . .

. . . if yellow feet ever reach American soil, yellow hands will clutch American women! Will that happen? That's largely up to you and the other redblooded young men of America.

Words won't stop them. Prayers won't stop them. The "other fellow" won't stop them. But YOU can stop them! You, with a hard-hitting Yankee rifle in your hands!

Every hour you delay you give those yellow hands the chance to draw closer to *your* sister . . . *your* wife . . . *your* sweetheart. Come on! JOIN UP NOW! Show them that you're *white* . . . that "*You're not yellow!*"

★

Join now!
you're <u>needed</u> now!

★

Proposed prototype for wartime advertising, 1938.

Typical World War II rape propaganda.

many historians whose fathers fought in the war might find evidence in family archives of the avidity with which soldiers collected pin-ups.[5]

Obviously, pin-ups functioned as surrogate sex objects for soldiers far from home, and I do not mean to discount this function. Soldiers viewed them as such, and some complained that the pin-ups in semi-official publications such as *Yank* were too tame. "I know you want to keep it clean," wrote one private to *Yank*, "but after all the boys are interested in sex, and *Esquire* and a few other magazines give us sex and still get by the mail, so why can't *Yank*?" They reacted bitterly to charges that pin-ups were immoral and to the threat of censorship. "Maybe if some of those 'panty waists' had to be stuck out some place where there are no white women and few native women for a year and a half, as we were," wrote some GIs in Alaska, "they would appreciate even a picture of our gals back home."[6]

American military officials linked the effective soldier's aggressiveness with healthy heterosexual desire and worried about sustaining such desire and thwarting homosexuality. Thus, it is plausible, as John D'Emilio and Estelle Freedman have said, that pin-ups were intended by the government to "encourage heterosexual fantasy in the sex-segregated military." Concerned also about epidemics of venereal disease, the government sought to provide activities in which sexual desire could be sublimated and even endorsed a measure of "autoeroticism," provided it did not become "habit-forming."[7]

But pin-ups were more than masturbatory aides. They also represented the private obligations for which soldiers were fighting. Several pieces of evidence suggest as much. First, many pin-ups were, as the complaints of some soldiers indicate, relatively demure. As Paul Fussell has said, they were hardly "triggers of lust," which is, in part, attributable to censorship: The War Department and Hollywood were willing to go only so far. Yet to attribute the limited erotic charge of pin-ups

James Westbrook in his Alaska barracks, 1943.

to censorship alone fails to explain why some of the most popular pin-ups were not those that flirted with the limits imposed by the censors. Above all, it fails to account for the appeal of far and away the most sought-after pin-up—Betty Grable. At one point, there were 20,000 requests per week for her pin-up, and by war's end it had been put in the hands of 5 million servicemen. This pin-up was modest compared with others such as runner-up Rita Hayworth, suggesting that servicemen viewed Grable and many of the other most popular pin-up models not only as objects of sexual fantasy but also as representative women, standing in for wives and sweethearts on the home front. "If I had a wife I would make sure her picture was up," one sailor remarked, "but Irene Manning will do until that big day." Reporting on behalf of the Hollywood Victory Committee, Alan Ladd observed in 1943 that those who had entertained the troops had learned that the boys preferred women who reminded them of their mothers and sisters. In search of "girls they can prize," servicemen were not interested in "flash." They preferred movies "whose components—street scenes, normal people on the streets, women who look like mothers, wives, sweethearts—bring them near home."[8]

Betty Grable's appeal, in particular, was less as an erotic "sex goddess" than as a symbol of the woman for whom American men—especially American working-class men—were fighting. She was the girl a man could prize. Her image, carefully cultivated by the star-making machinery of Twentieth Century Fox, was "straight-arrow, chintz-table-cloth." Darryl Zanuck, the head of the studio, correctly guessed that Grable would appeal to soldiers, and he featured her in a series of Technicolor musicals that highlighted her "pastel charms." In her movies, Grable repeatedly portrayed a young woman tempted by "flash" but, in the end, claimed for gentility. In *Pin-Up Girl* (1944), for example, she played Laurie Jones, a local pin-up girl popular with the soldiers at the USO Club in Missoula, Missouri, who possesses a vivid imagination and a weakness for the white lie. After moving to Washington to take a job as a government stenographer, Laurie attempts to win the heart of Guadalcanal hero Tommy Dooley by pretending that she is glamorous showgirl Laura Lorraine, only to discover that what Tommy really wants and needs is a girl like the real Laurie Jones: "sincere, honest, with both feet on the ground." In the film's finale, she reveals that Laurie Jones and Laura Lorraine are one and the same woman and accepts herself as she is: a level-headed, small-town girl who happens to know her way around an elaborate production number.[9]

This reading of Grable's appeal is not to deny a sexual dimension to her popularity. It is rather to situate her sexuality within a configuration of attributes that established her as a principal icon of obligation. Grable's sexiness was, as condescending middlebrow critics often

Betty Grable, pin-up queen.

Rita Hayworth, pin-up runner-up.

sneered, "of the common sort"—and this was a key to her success. Almost everyone, including Grable herself, agreed that, as *Time* put it, "she can lay no claims to sultry beauty or mysterious glamour. . . . Her peach-cheeked, pearl blonde good looks add up to mere candybox-top prettiness." If we place Grable's image within the discourse of obligation as well as that of soft-core pornography, we can explain how it flourished despite bucking what Andre Bazin perceived as a drift of the American male gaze during the war from the leg to the breast. By these lights, Grable's standing as the premier pin-up girl is inexplicable, given that her legs were said to be her most striking attribute. Of course, Bazin might have been wrong, and Grable's popularity, compared with Rita Hayworth's and Jane Russell's, might merely indicate that "leg-men" still outnumbered "breast-men" during the war. Yet this conclusion, I think, is too simple. Even Grable's legs were celebrated less for their exceptional beauty than for their "average" look. As *Life* reported, Grable's legs—"her private trademark"—were venerated not as extraordinary but as "the Great American Average Legs: straight, perfectly rounded and shaped, but withal judged by the same standards as millions of others."[10]

Finally, one must not forget that the war in the Pacific was a race war, and Grable's obvious "whiteness" gave her an advantage over competitors such as Hayworth (née Margarita Cansino) in the eyes of white soldiers waging a brutal struggle against a racial enemy in a setting where, as they often complained, white women—especially women as white as Grable—were in short supply. As *Time* reported, soldiers preferred Grable to other pin-ups "in direct ratio to their remoteness from civilization." Here again, in a nation still firmly in the grip of white supremacy, Betty Grable provided the superior image of American womanhood.[11]

Packaged as the serviceman's favorite, Grable quickly caught on as such. No one received more fan mail from soldiers, and by the end of the war she was the most popular star in Hollywood, earning the largest salary of any woman in America. Summing up the attitude they held toward her, one veteran told Grable: "There we were out in those damn dirty trenches. Machine guns firing. Bombs dropping all around us. We would be exhausted, frightened, confused and some-

Sad Sack suffers from the shortage of white women in the Pacific.

times hopeless about our situation. When suddenly someone would pull your picture out of his wallet. Or we'd see a decal of you on a plane and then we'd *know* what we were fighting for." In October 1943 *Modern Screen* reported that a soldier had died clutching Grable's photograph. If, as Richard Schickel scoffed, she was "democratic womanhood's lowest common denominator," it was precisely for this reason that she came to represent those worth dying for. "In her time," as Jane Gaines has said, Grable was "model girlfriend, wife, and finally mother." Indeed, her popularity increased after she married band-leader Harry James in 1943 and had a child later that year. She fared as well, if not better, as "pin-up mamma" as she had as "pin-up girl."[12]

Perhaps the most striking evidence of how pin-ups functioned as part of wartime discourse about obligation is the plastering of images of Grable and others to the machines of war, where they competed with and upstaged the insignias of the state. As John Costello has observed, "By 1945 there was hardly a tank or a plane in the U.S. military that was not adorned with its own painted icon of femininity as a good-luck talisman that also showed the enemy what it was that red-blooded Americans 'were fighting for.'" This practice was not just a matter of naming planes after girls (or of comparing girls to planes) but of removing the obfuscating veil of arguments for a soldier's obligation to die for the liberal state to reveal (nakedly) the private obligations upon which such states ultimately relied.[13]

In suggesting that pin-ups involved more than sexual exploitation and that they advanced a tacit moral argument, I do not mean to endorse that argument. It is a troubling one. In an acute discussion of the asymmetrical relationship between "protector" and "protected," Judith Hicks Stiehm has observed that this argument assigns women to the role of the "protected" simply by virtue of their gender.

Moreover, this argument has some disturbing effects on male protectors. Men, who alone can use violent power, find their identity bound up with the effectiveness of the protection they provide to their dependents. Hence, they may tend to "overprotect" them, and, even more disturbing, "the protector [tends] to become a predator" who turns on his dependents, especially when things go badly.

> When there is no real work or duty required of a protector, the role is satisfying, it makes one proud. As the role demands increase, and/or as the chances of fulfilling the role decrease, the practice of the role becomes less and less attractive. The protected become a nuisance, a burden, and finally a shame, for an unprotected protectee is the clearest possible evidence of a protector's failure. As one gains ascendancy, one gains dependents, as one gains dependents their requirements for protection increase. Thus the most wholly dependent protectees may be just the ones most likely to trigger a nihilistic impulse in their protector.

Jane Russell admires "her" plane.

The dynamic that Stiehm describes may help explain why so much literature that soldiers produced, which critics such as Susan Gubar have analyzed, is often violently misogynistic. Though pin-ups are not the best documents through which to explore this dynamic, the use of a Grable pin-up to instruct troops in map reading contains a hint of it. This device was said to be an aid to concentration, but it also seems to "target" Grable's anatomy, in which case Grable's image proved eminently adaptable to expressing the darker side of the pressing obligations connecting men and women during the war.[14]

Betty Grable teaches map reading.

The obligation to be worthy of protection. Palmolive Soap advertisement, 1943.

Though male soldiers were the principal collectors of pin-ups, the pin-up girl also addressed herself to American women, suggesting that if men were obliged to fight for their pin-up girls, women were in turn obliged to fashion themselves into pin-up girls worth fighting for. Pin-ups, that is, argued for a reciprocal obligation. Amidst a call to women to do their part by taking up (for the duration) the jobs that men had left behind, they were also obliged to be women their men would be proud to protect.[15]

Here too Betty Grable was an important figure. She was admired by women as well as men. Her rise to box-office champion during the war was the result of the women who flocked to her movies as much as to the soldiers who pinned her up overseas. "Girls can see me in a picture," she said, "and feel I could be one of them." During the war, she was offered to women—especially working-class women—as a model of female virtue on the home front. "Men are so right about everything, especially Betty Grable," declared *Photoplay*. "Girls who want to be brides should aim to be like Betty." Young working-class women avidly followed Grable's career in the fan magazines, where her domestic life, as they portrayed it, was held up as an example to readers. As Gaines says, "Even though Grable was making a six-figure yearly salary, in the fan magazines she was still the little family budget-keeper, living within her million-dollar means and outfitting the ranch house with bargains from the Sears catalogue." Above all, it was Grable's self-effacing modesty that recommended her to women. Advising her readers on how to please men, she said, "Remember to follow their lead, from dancing to conversation. Talk about *them*. The most popular girls at the Hollywood Canteen, for instance, are the really good listeners: the ones who hang on to a man's words as if he were the Oracle of War and the only person in the room." Betty Grable, *Photoplay* observed, "is as modest as the girl who married Dad."[16]

Pin-up sent by Rita Weinberg to Bernie Kessel, *Life*, 30 November 1942.

It is important, of course, to assess the extent to which American women felt the obligation to be pin-ups men would die for, but finding such evidence is much more difficult. I can only say that what evidence I have been able to gather suggests that many women took this obligation to heart. American soldiers marched into battle with pin-ups not only of Betty Grable but also of their own wives and girl-friends. Grable both explicitly and by example urged women who thought they looked good in a bathing suit to send a snapshot to servicemen, and many heeded her advice. Like Rita Weinberg of the Bronx, thousands of American women provided soldiers like Bernie Kessel with photographs to tuck in their helmets and pin to their weapons, and in these photographs women often expertly constructed their images using pin-up conventions: the one-piece bathing suit or sweater, high heels, the over-the-shoulder look, the "pleasing convexities" of the bent knee, and the bright, coy, "come on" smile. Even my mother, I must say, proved adept at this, carefully tailoring her photographic image to conventions established by Lana Turner and others.

Moreover, though homemade cheesecake circulated as widely as the Hollywood variety on the battlefront, soldiers often opted for apple pie instead. As the American Expeditionary Force gathered in Northern Ireland in 1942 for the invasion of North Africa, they held a contest for the "Sweetheart of the AEF," and the winner was Janet ("Angel") Barry of Belmar, New Jersey—a pin-up at which even George Bush might in good conscience have sneaked a peek.[17]

Living Theory

Occasionally, citizens recognize that political theory involves more than the labor of those specialists called political theorists and realize that in their everyday experience as citizens they live theory. During a war, when they ask "why we fight," representatives of the state supply them with answers that best serve the interests of the state, and citizens often accept these answers, which accord with their own sense of where their obligations lie, a sense developed within the confines of a particular political culture.

Because the public life in a liberal political culture such as that of the United States is thin, modern American statesmen and their allies have found it difficult to call upon their fellow citizens *as citizens* to defend their nation in time of war. Though given to justify wars on behalf of principles transcending the values of any particular political community, they also have legitimated the sacrifices of war by relying heavily on appeals to private (which is not to say selfish) obligations,

Nancy (Gillam) Westbrook's homemade pin-up, 1945.

including the moral commitments believed to exist between men and women. These arguments are sometimes explicit; often they are not. As living theory, they can be found in some unexpected places, even in pin-ups.

Given the centrality of the mutual obligations, both prescribed and felt, between men and women to American mobilization during World War II, it is not surprising that pin-ups were sanctioned by the state. Nor is it surprising that the photograph that has come to signify

Lana Turner, 1941.

the end of American participation in the war portrays the consumma-
tion of the bargain between protector and protected. In Times Square
in August 1945, *Life* photographer Alfred Eisenstaedt captured a protector exacting his reward from a woman he grabbed on the street, a
representative of the protected who happened to be close at hand. Apparently this sailor shared the conviction of fellow soldiers in New
Guinea who, earlier in the war, had remarked that "we are not only
fighting for the Four Freedoms, we are fighting also for the priceless
privilege of making love to American women."[18] Having helped win

Janet "Angel" Barry, "Sweetheart of the AEF," *Life*, 30 November 1942.

The ambiguities of protection—sailor kissing nurse in Times Square on VJ Day, *Life*, 27 August 1945.

that fight, the sailor and other soldiers returned home to reap the rewards they believed were their due. If I am right about the character of American discourse concerning obligation during World War II, it is fitting to mark the end of the "Good War" with a representative kiss, manifesting in its mix of joy and violence the ambiguities of the moral contract binding protective men and protected women in a liberal state.

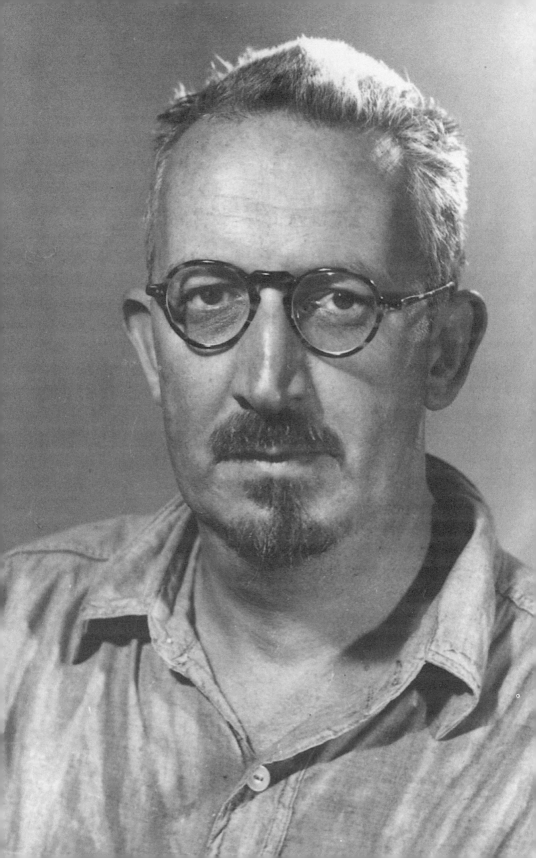

The Responsibility of Peoples

Dwight Macdonald and the Holocaust

When news of the full measure of the Nazis' crimes against European Jews finally broke through the barriers of disbelief and indifference in the latter months of World War II, most Americans reacted with bewildered horror. Alfred Kazin evoked this moment powerfully in the concluding passage of his memoir, *Starting Out in the Thirties*:

One day in the spring of 1945, when the war against Hitler was almost won, I sat in a newsreel theater in Piccadilly looking at the first films of newly liberated Belsen. On the screen, sticks in black-and-white prison garb leaned on a wire, staring dreamily at the camera. Other sticks shuffled about, or sat vaguely on

Dwight Macdonald, editor of *Politics* and keen
observer of the war's moral temper.

the ground, next to an enormous pile of bodies, piled up like cordwood, from which protruded legs, arms, heads. A few guards were collected sullenly in a corner, and for a moment a British Army bulldozer was shown digging an enormous hole in the ground. Then the sticks would come back on the screen, hanging on the wire, looking at us. It was un-bearable. People coughed in embarrassment, and in embarrassment many laughed.

For Kazin, the Holocaust marked an end to "the radical confidence of the 1930s." It was, he said, "the nightmare that would bring everything else into question, that will haunt me to my last breath."[1]

For American intellectuals, Kazin observed, the Holocaust posed special horrors:

> The faster time carried us away from it, the closer the gas came. It stole up our skin without our always knowing it. It was *total*, the inescapable crime lying across the most documented century in history. . . . The abyss was at our feet because we believed in nothing so much as what [Lionel] Trilling called "the life of the mind." The life of the mind was of no use unless it addressed itself to the gas. . . . Nothing else was serious. Murder had become the first political principle. We had to recognize the abyss on whose edge we lived.[2]

On the basis of retrospective accounts such as this (which is not at all idiosyncratic), one would expect to find an outpouring of critical reflection by American intellectuals on the implications of the Holo-caust for the life of the mind. Moreover, one would expect such re-flection to be particularly prominent in the work of the "New York intellectuals" (of which Kazin was a part), a group of intellectuals, most of them Jewish, who had by the late forties begun to move to the forefront of American cultural life, establishing one of the few intelligentsias in the country's history.[3]

The reality, however, falls a good deal short of these expectations. The New York intellectuals' response to the Holocaust was, with a few notable exceptions, slow to come and, when it did come, it was "limited and oblique."[4] During the war and immediately after, *Partisan Review*, which has been accurately described as "the very voice and soul of the New York intelligentsia," was virtually silent about the destruction of the Jews. The other principal journal of these intellectuals in the 1940s, *Commentary*, which began publication in November 1945 under the auspices of the American Jewish Committee, did provide its readers with valuable documents and accounts of the Holocaust and lengthy reviews of early books by survivors. Nonetheless, although the shadow of Nazi terror hung over nearly everything published in this magazine during its early years, few of its contributors ventured beyond describing the horrors of the "war against the Jews" toward trying to understand that war's meaning and implications. Ten years after the end of World War II, *Commentary* reviewer Solomon Bloom commented on this continuing silence, noting that "the facts are incontrovertible, yet it is easier to believe that these things have happened than that they could have happened. The senses cry truth, but the mind hesitates, for it can see only through understanding."[5] Not until the explosive controversy over Hannah Arendt's *Eichmann in Jerusalem* in 1963 would many New York intellectuals directly and openly confront this problem of understanding.

Suffering and Silence

Hannah Arendt was one of two major exceptions to this generalization; the other was Dwight Macdonald. In any discussion of the New York intellectuals and the Holocaust, Arendt will be at center stage, and I do not intend to displace her by calling attention to Macdonald's often-neglected effort to make sense of the Nazi's crimes. When *The Origins of Totalitarianism* was published in 1951, Macdonald himself hailed Arendt as "the most original and profound—therefore the most valuable—political theoretician of our times," comparing her demystification of totalitarianism to Marx's analysis of capitalism.[6]

Relatively modest though it may be, however, Macdonald's work does merit more attention than it has received. In the waning days of World War II, he was the only New York intellectual, other than Arendt, to directly confront the implications of the unique terrors of that conflict, and his long essay titled "The Responsibility of Peoples," published in March 1945, stands as the single attempt by a long-standing member of this community to understand the Holocaust in the 1940s. During the late forties, his thinking closely paralleled Arendt's, and they shared a set of interests and insights.[7]

Before examining Macdonald's effort to understand something of the meaning and implications of the Holocaust, it is important to sketch the reasons for the limited response of other New York intellectuals. In this context, Macdonald's unusually ready effort to address his mind to the gas will become more explicable. In his memoir, *Margin of Hope,* Irving Howe offered three general arguments for understanding the tardy and indirect reaction of most New York intellectuals to the Holocaust. These arguments do not, as Howe admitted, amount to an effective apologia, but, taken together, they do make a compelling explanation.[8]

First, the Holocaust's horrors were simply unprecedented. As Howe said,

> People don't react to great cataclysms with clear thought and eloquent
> emotions; they blink and stumble, they retreat to old opinions, they turn

away in fear. . . . To be human meant to be unequipped to grapple with the Holocaust. We had no precedents in thought or experience. . . . We had no metaphors that could release the work of the imagination. All efforts to understand what had happened in Europe required as their premise a wrenching away from received categories of thought—but that cannot happen overnight, it isn't easy to check in your modest quantity of mental stock.[9]

Similar statements of baffled intellectual impotence are in abundant evidence in the 1940s. Indeed, what little public response the New York intellectuals offered to the Holocaust were most often reflections on their inability to respond. "The great psychological fact of our time which we all observe with baffled wonder and shame," Lionel Trilling remarked, "is that there is no possible way of responding to Belsen and Buchenwald. The activity of mind fails before the incommunicability of man's suffering." Sometimes the reflections on this failure could, as in the case of Isaac Rosenfeld, be powerful and moving:

We still don't understand what happened to the Jews of Europe, and perhaps we never will. There have been books, magazine and newspaper articles, eyewitness accounts, letters, diaries, documents certified by the highest authorities on the life in ghettos and concentration camps, slave factories and extermination centers under the Germans. By now we know all there is to know, but it hasn't helped; we still don't understand. . . . There is nothing but numbness, and in the respect of numbness we . . . are no different from the murderers who went ahead and did their business and paid no attention to the screams.[10]

This response to the crimes of the Nazis is understandable, and, no doubt, as Howe suggested, helps to explain the limited engagement of most intellectuals with these crimes. Nevertheless, as he said, it is not a sufficient explanation, for there were those in the forties who did go beyond bewildered numbness toward understanding and explanation. Arendt (who quoted Rosenfeld's remark approvingly), argued that it was the "fearful anticipation" of one who dreaded "the concentration camp as a possibility for the future" that drove her "to keep thinking about horrors," and the same can be said of Macdonald. But it could also said of most of the New York intellectuals, who quickly came to share Arendt's contention that "the most essential political criterion for judging the events of our time" was, "Will it lead to totalitarian rule or will it not?" There is no evidence that Arendt and Macdonald felt the numbness any less or that other intellectuals felt less urgently what Bloom termed "the mandate to penetrate and account for this extraordinary crime," but the fact remains that they responded differently. For many, as Karla Goldman has said, "the difficulty of finding an adequate response translated into no response at all."[11]

A second important factor limiting the response of many New York intellectuals to the Holocaust was their residual Marxism. Although most had been firmly anti-Stalinist since the midthirties, many remained wedded in the forties to Marxist categories for their analysis of the social and political world, and Marxism could not explain the Holocaust. Marxism, Howe observed, "kept us from seeing the radically novel particulars of the Nazi regime. Neither the political course nor economic laws nor social psychology of bourgeois society could begin to explain what had happened at Auschwitz." Marxist analysis of the Third Reich tended to treat anti-Semitism as an ideology designed to distract the German masses from the solid alliance the Nazis had forged between big business and the state. Such an analysis could explain neither the ascendancy of the Final Solution among German war aims nor the diabolical form this solution took. "The internal political value of anti-Semitism," Franz Neumann asserted wrongly in his classic Marxist study of Nazism, *Behemoth*, "will never allow a complete extermination of the Jews." Marxism, like all theories built on the logic of rational human interests, was mute in the face of the death camp.[12]

The final circumstance shaping the oblique response of these American intellectuals to the Final Solution was that, for many of them, coming to terms with the Holocaust meant coming to terms with their identity as Jews, a process that was protracted, difficult, and, for the most part, unpublicized. Because this interaction between the Holocaust and self-identification was a private and, in some respects, unconscious development, being precise about its dynamics is difficult, but there is ready testimony to its importance.

Until the midforties, secularism and cosmopolitanism were badges of pride among the New York intellectuals. "Their faith," as Kazin put it, "was to be 'intellectuals.'"[13] The Holocaust created an uneasiness about this universalistic faith, an uneasiness evident in the contributions of young Jewish intellectuals to a symposium published by the *Contemporary Jewish Record* in February 1944. Particularly striking were the comments of Lionel Trilling, who was at the time well on his way to establishing himself as the paradigmatic cosmopolitan Jewish American intellectual. "I cannot discover anything in my professional intellectual life which I can specifically trace back to my Jewish birth and rearing," he said. Trilling was willing only to affirm the minimal "point of honor" that "I would not, even if I could, deny or escape being Jewish," a position, he admitted, that "hangs upon only a resistance (and even only a passive one) to the stupidity and brutality which make the Jewish situation so bad as it is." This minimal position, he noted, "has, I suppose, a certain gracelessness—if only because millions of Jews are suffering simply because they have the heritage that I so minimalize in my own intellectual life." Nonetheless, Trilling warned against the "mere guilty gesture." "Suffering does not confer virtue," he concluded. "I know of no writer in English who has added a micro-millimetre to his stature by 'realizing his Jewishness,' although I know of some who have curtailed their promise by trying to heighten their Jewish consciousness."[14] Thus, although by war's end few of the New York intellectuals denied the contention of *Commentary* editor Elliot Cohen that "one is a Jew because, after Hitler and the six million exterminated, how can one repudiate the bond?" it was unclear in 1945 what form, if any, the bond would take beyond Trilling's minimal point of honor.[15]

By the late forties, it was evident that for some intellectuals the bond would revive interest in Jewish traditions and, in some instances, even a rapprochement with the American Jewish community, whose culture they had for years compared to "the rigor mortis of an Elks Convention." Study groups were formed to read the Torah and Maimonides, and *Commentary* published classical and modern religious texts in a regular section titled "Cedars of Lebanon." Critics like Leslie Fiedler, Irving Kristol, and Harold Rosenberg offered interpretations of traditional literature, and many shared Kristol's affirmation that after 5,000 years, he was not prepared to see Judaism die with him.[16]

Not all New York intellectuals shared this enthusiasm for a revival of traditional Judaism. Howe characterized it as "a sickeningly sentimental business" and a "sheer phony, self-induced, uncritical nostalgia for something that never existed as they imagine it." Sidney Hook, ever the Deweyan naturalist, labeled the interest in religious orthodoxy a "new failure of nerve" and chided "some young literary Jewish intellectuals who, looking enviously at the Church, are prepared to join the synagogue if only Kafka is added to the Apocryphal books of the Old Testament." A good deal can be said for such criticism, but, whatever one thinks of its substance, for some New York intellectuals this new interest in Judaism as a religion was an important, albeit indirect, way of confronting the Holocaust.[17]

This new sense of Jewish identity quickly began to make itself felt in the internecine quarrels that marked this intelligentsia's cultural politics. Perhaps the clearest indicator of the change that the Holocaust had engendered in many New York intellectuals' self-definition was the controversy surrounding the award of the Bollingen Prize for poetry to Ezra Pound in 1949. Many protested that Pound's work as an anti-Semitic propagandist in Italy during the war disqualified him for the honor. Some writers and critics opposed the award explicitly as Jews. "As a Jew," Clement Greenberg declared, "I myself cannot help being offended by the matter of Pound's latest poetry. And since 1943 things like that make me physically afraid too." Karl Shapiro, one of the Bollingen judges, revealed that the "first and most crucial reason" he had voted against awarding the prize to Pound was that "I am a Jew and cannot honor antisemites." Such sentiments were significant not only because they evidenced a newfound ethnic self-consciousness but also because they challenged the New York intellectuals' long-standing defense of modernists like Pound and T. S. Eliot despite these poets' reactionary politics. After the Holocaust, however, this community of discourse no longer took for granted the principle that "a poet's technical accomplishments can transform material that is ugly and vicious into beautiful poetry."[18]

A word should be said, finally, about an apparently very direct engagement with the Holocaust by the New York intellectuals: their championing use of "totalitarianism" as a tool for social analysis and political understanding during the cold war. In 1949, Elliot Cohen argued that "it is the [intellectual's] special experience as a Jew, in which the concentration camp is the culmination and symbol, that is a chief factor in his present central preoccupation with totalitarianism; and it is because of his Jewish position in society that he continues to find himself in a kind of strategic center of this whole question." Logical as this proposition sounds, I think it gets the story backward in most cases. It was not the Holocaust that enabled the New York intellectuals to come to terms with totalitarianism but the concept of totalitarianism that enabled them to confront the Holocaust in a peculiarly "oblique and sublimated" fashion. The New York intellectuals had been preoccupied with totalitarianism since the midthirties, when their belief in the "fearful symmetry" between the Nazi and Soviet regimes animated their anti-Stalinism. The Holocaust did little to alter or redirect this understanding. Indeed, in one respect the Final Solution could not be assimilated into the prevailing concept of totalitarianism without depriving that concept of much of its power as a tool of comparative political analysis and cold war politics. That is, focusing on the Nazis' racism and their "war against the Jews" would have highlighted those particularistic, substantive aspects of the Nazi belief system that distinguished it from Stalinism rather than those formal features that these "total ideologies" shared. What is noteworthy, *pace* Cohen, is how little effect the Holocaust had on the New York intellectuals' concept of totalitarianism. The concept, in all its imposing abstractness and formalism, did, however, enable these intellectuals to incorporate the Holocaust into their political worldview while distancing them from the particular horrors that bore on their newfound and still ambivalent identity as Jews. As Howe says, it "was easier to talk about the nature of totalitarian society than to confront the Holocaust."[19]

Ironically, it was Arendt who provided her fellow New York intellectuals with one of the most formidable and abstract formulations of the concept in her widely hailed study, *The Origins of Totalitarianism.*

For Arendt, the Nazis' crimes against the Jews were in their most important aspect "crimes against humanity" rather than crimes against the Jewish people. For her, as Daniel Bell noted, "it is the *act* not the *victim* which is salient."[20] Moreover, her "politics of fearful anticipation" by its very nature called for a general concept of totalitarianism abstracted from the unique historical particulars that distinguished one instance of genocidal terror from another. History would not repeat itself, but Arendt warned, totalitarianism might well reappear in new forms, directing its terrible logic at different victims for different ends. Those who focused on Nazi anti-Semitism, she feared, would be unprepared to meet this threat.

Whatever one thinks of Arendt's arguments, her abstractions were not ready-made but wrung from a travail of understanding that few other American intellectuals ventured. Arendt's warm, respectful, almost worshipful reception into the New York intellectual community grew in part out of her exceptional attempt to understand the Holocaust. They loved her, Kazin said, because "she gave her friends intellectual courage before the moral terror the war had willed to us."[21]

In 1963, however, when Arendt applied rigorous standards of universal, abstract justice not only to Adolf Eichmann but also to the Jewish elites that he had integrated into his bureaucratic machine of mass extermination and to the state of Israel's conduct of his trial, she found herself at the center of a bitter controversy. Arendt drew fire not only from those critics who questioned her judgments on her own terms but also from those intellectuals who had discovered the virtues of a parochial identity and, as a consequence, questioned the "cold objectivity" of her universalistic, cosmopolitan standards themselves. Arendt's *Eichmann in Jerusalem* finally provoked a direct confrontation with the Holocaust by intellectuals who, as Bell put it, had come to believe that "in this situation, one's identity as a Jew, as well as *philosophe*, is relevant." Arendt's failure to perceive this, Marie Syrkin (among others) charged, explained why she was "able not only to distort the facts but—more important—to fail so signally in sympathy and imagination." Thus the "cry of Jewish grief" that Irving Howe said should have been the first response of the New York intellectuals to the Holocaust was finally heard, and it was directed at one of their own.[22]

Explaining Macdonald

Dwight Macdonald was one of Arendt's staunchest supporters in the Eichmann controversy. His support reflected not only his respect and affection for her but also his own perspective on the Holocaust that he had articulated in the dark days when the Nazis' "terrible secret" was unveiled.[23]

Beginning in 1944, the vehicle for Macdonald's writing was *Politics*, a magazine he founded following his departure from the *Partisan Review* editorial board because editors Philip Rahv and William Phillips disputed his political opposition to World War II. Although much of the writing in *Politics* was Macdonald's own (he was owner, publisher, and editor, and his wife, Nancy, was business manager), its major contributors included Americans Lionel Abel, Daniel Bell, Paul Goodman, Irving Howe, Mary McCarthy, and C. Wright Mills, and émigrés and Europeans Bruno Bettelheim, Albert Camus, Nicola Chiaromonte, Lewis Coser, Victor Serge, and Simone Weil. *Politics* was published for only five years (1944–49), and it never achieved a circulation of more than 5,000. These figures, however, do not reflect its significance, for in the forties, as Daniel Bell has observed, "*Politics* was the only magazine that was aware of and insistently kept calling attention to, changes that were taking place in moral temper, the depths of which we still incompletely realize." Nowhere was this more evident than in Macdonald's effort to understand the altered conditions of moral responsibility after the Holocaust.[24]

Before I analyze his signal essay, "The Responsibility of Peoples," let me note briefly the circumstances that help explain why Macdonald was able, as many others were not, to engage the Holocaust so directly. Some of these circumstances are simply the reverse of those that explain the muted response of other New York intellectuals, some are more complex.

Most obvious is the simple fact that Macdonald was not Jewish, and, for this reason, coming to terms with the Holocaust was not for him bound up with issues of personal identity. He was not unaware that this was a problem for others, but he found it troubling. The "postwar reaction of Jews to death camps," he noted, "was to become collectively conscious as Jews—understandable but dismaying to a non-Jew." In the late forties, Macdonald's rigorous cosmopolitanism and his hostility to what he termed "semitism" among some of his friends led to some nasty confrontations in which Clement Greenberg and others charged him with anti-Semitism. He celebrated the Bollingen award to Pound as "the brightest political act in a dark period" and correctly complained to critics that in saying so he was simply adhering to the separation of aesthetic and political judgment that New York intellectuals had practiced since the 1930s.[25] Later, during the Eichmann controversy, Macdonald did not go as far as Mary McCarthy, who (wrongly) claimed that Arendt's supporters and critics were divided between Gentiles and Jews, but he did suggest that hostile reviews were "motivated less by rationality than by Jewish patriotism." He chided those who criticized Arendt's universalism, and he speculated perceptively that "it is an interesting, and depressing, historical exercise to imagine what the reactions would have been to a book like this in the thirties, when all of us . . . despised national and racial feelings and were hot for truth, justice and other universals."[26]

By 1945 Macdonald was also well along his way toward renouncing the Marxism that inhibited many intellectuals' response to the Holocaust. Hounded out of the Trotskyists in 1941 for his heretical view of Nazism not as the final stage of monopoly capitalism but as a new form of society that he called "bureaucratic collectivism," Macdonald was steadily weaning himself in the early forties from the deterministic Marxist faith in progressive history, a process that would culminate in 1946 in his lengthy critique of this ideology, "The Root Is Man." He also chastised Marxist critics of "The Responsibility of Peoples" for failing to recognize that what the Nazis had done was beyond anything that a nineteenth-century doctrine like Marxism ("so rational, so materialistic, so convinced of 'progress' etc.") could imagine.[27]

Macdonald's antiwar politics also nourished his critical thinking. He initially opposed the war on the more or less Trotskyist grounds that the war was a conflict of competing imperialisms in which radicals should support neither the Allies nor the Axis but rather work to foment a revolutionary, working-class "third camp" that would take advantage of the chaos of war to defeat the ruling classes of all the major powers. This position Macdonald would later say was fantastic and a mistake. It was, however, a "creative mistake" because it freed him to openly criticize the phenomenon of total war itself. As Macdonald anticipated, radical intellectuals who lent their "critical support" to the Allies provided a good deal of support but little criticism; his former colleagues at *Partisan Review* were simply silent. By the time he began publishing *Politics*, Macdonald was focusing less on the question of the war's justness (*jus ad bellum*) than on the issues raised by how the war was being fought on all sides (*jus in bello*). The analysis of "War as an Institution"—the title of a series of articles Macdonald launched in 1944—was among the most important features of the early issues of *Politics*, and the perspective he was developing on modern war as "rationality and system gone mad" served him in good stead when he turned his attention to the Holocaust.[28]

Because Macdonald did not retreat from radical politics during the war, he was more directly in touch with political events in Europe than most other American intellectuals. He kept close tabs on the refugee situation and on the resistance movements in Europe. Indeed, because so many of its contributors were Europeans or émigrés, *Politics* was virtually a Euro-American magazine, and its contributors shared the worldview of the libertarian radicals in the European resistance. Hoping as they did that the war would bring about the radical reconstruction of European society, the *Politics* circle was almost an American outpost of the resistance. As Macdonald noted, the magazine was "a kind of transplanted spore of European culture growing in an environment that is physically and politically more favorable to free thought than that of modern Europe."[29]

In explaining Macdonald's ready response to the Holocaust, one also should not underestimate the his instincts as a journalist. The destruction of the Jews was an important "story," and, at bottom, Macdonald had the sensibility of a great journalist. This did not always win him the admiration of other New York intellectuals, who regarded him as a naïf in matters of high theory and regularly questioned the "seriousness" of his writing. Nevertheless, the Holocaust was an event that a good reporter could not pass up, and it was a story ideally suited to the blend of concrete reportage and moral reflection that marked Macdonald's best work.[30]

Finally, and perhaps most important, Macdonald could respond directly to Nazi crimes because he had developed, as many New York intellectuals had not, a self-consciously moral outlook on politics. He did not regard ethics as mere "ideology," and for this he suffered a good deal of abuse from "hard-boiled" intellectuals who charged him with fleeing from the "realities" of power into "an empyrean of moral rectitude and passivity, transcending the uproars and skirmishes of the political arena." Macdonald refused to accept the distinction that this implies between politics and morality, choosing to align himself, he said, with those from Plato to Weber who had argued that relating ethics to politics was "the most significant task which political thought can accomplish." Abandoning this task just because the difficulties involved had not been resolved satisfactorily, he wryly remarked, was akin to abandoning poetry just because no one had solved the problem of creating a perfect poem.[31]

Macdonald shared Arendt's belief that the terror of the Holocaust was above all a moral terror: the Nazis had committed crimes against "the very nature of mankind." In the face of these numbing and unprecedented horrors he, like Arendt, sought in the first instance simply to explain their strangeness. Both aimed, as Arendt said, "not to give answers but rather to prepare the ground."[32] The Holocaust posed stark and bewildering problems of politics and ethics, and Macdonald intended not so much to solve these problems as to understand why the conventional categories of moral and political analysis could not adequately contain them.

Mad Logic

Macdonald succinctly summarized this concern in the opening sentences of "The Responsibility of Peoples":

> Something has happened to the Germans—to some of them, at least; something has happened to Europe—to some of it, at least. What is it?

Who or what is responsible? What does it mean about our civilization, our whole system of values? This is the great moral question of our times, and on what our hearts as well as our heads answer to it depends largely our answer to the great practical questions.[33]

Unlike Arendt, who focused on the nature of the Holocaust ("what is it?"), Macdonald centered on the issue of responsibility. He did, however, briefly consider the character of Nazi crimes, concluding with Arendt that they were in important respects unique and unprecedented. In so doing, he began to move toward a concept of totalitarianism similar to hers.

What was unique about exterminating the Jews, Macdonald argued, was that the Nazis pursued the Final Solution as an end in itself. It was an action utterly lacking in utility in any conventional sense; it escaped any prevailing notion of "war crimes."

> The extermination of the Jews of Europe was not a means to any end one can accept as even plausibly rational. The Jews of Europe were murdered to gratify a paranoiac hatred . . . but for no reason of policy or advantage that I can see. . . . There was no ulterior motive behind Maidanek, no possible advantage to its creators beyond the gratification of neurotic race hatreds. What has previously been done only by individual psychopathic killers has now been done by the rulers and servants of a great modern State. This is something new (84–85).

This analysis of the Holocaust's uniqueness troubled some of Macdonald's readers. Both Solomon Bloom and Gordon Clough suggested that, given the Nazi goal of racial domination and the threat they perceived the Jews to present to this goal, exterminating the Jews was "rational"; that is, extermination was technically or instrumentally rational. It was a logical (if horrible) means to the end.[34] Macdonald's response to these readers was confusing. At first he seemed to say that it was the Nazis' ends, those dictated by their racial theories, that were irrational, however rational the means they used to realize these ends. "The death camps were rational in terms of the plan," he noted, "but what of the plan itself?" However, when he proceeded to argue this point further, Macdonald shifted his ground, questioning not the substantive rationality of Nazi race theory but the technical rationality of extermination as a means to racial domination. It would have been more rational, he said, for the Nazis to enslave rather than exterminate the Jews.[35] This confusion in Macdonald's argument suggests that he had not quite grasped the Final Solution's terrifying combination of irrationality and logic. As Arendt wrote,

> If we assume that most of our actions are of a utilitarian nature and that our evil deeds spring from some "exaggeration" of self-interest, then we are forced to conclude that [the death camp] is beyond human understanding. If, on the other hand, we make an abstraction of every standard we usually live by and consider only the fantastic ideological claims of racism in its logical purity, then the extermination of the Nazis makes almost too much sense. Behind its horrors lies the same inflexible logic which is characteristic of certain systems of paranoiacs where everything follows with absolute necessity once the first insane premise is accepted.[36]

In his initial point about the bizarre character of Nazi ends, Macdonald seemed to be reaching for a conception similar to Arendt's of Nazism as a "total ideology"—a grandiose design to "reshape men to fit into a rigid, logical, abstract dreamworld," an irrational though internally consistent anti-utopia. His subsequent thrashing about suggests that in 1945 he was as yet unable to move conclusively beyond the utilitarian premises that Arendt claimed would forever inhibit an adequate understanding of the Holocaust, but he was advancing steadily toward this dark territory of analysis.[37]

Collective Guilt

In "The Responsibility of Peoples," Macdonald sought to challenge the attribution of "collective guilt" to the German people for Nazi war crimes. This sentiment was widespread in 1945, and it was embodied at the policy level in Secretary of the Treasury Henry Morgenthau's plan to deindustrialize Germany after the war. It was, moreover, not a notion confined to conservatives. The British Trade Union Congress had overwhelmingly endorsed a resolution blaming the German people for Nazi crimes, and the CIO had declared at its annual convention that "the German people must atone for the crimes and horrors which they have visited on the earth" (93).[38]

Macdonald admitted at the outset of his essay that not all notions of collective responsibility were equally worthless. He would, he said, hold a people responsible for collective actions taken in accord with its folkways. "If we can conceive of a modern people as collectively responsible in a moral sense at all, then it must be held accountable only for actions which it takes spontaneously and as a whole, actions which are approved by the popular mores. It cannot be indicted for things done by sharply differentiated sub-groups" (85). An example of this, he argued, was acts of violence against Negroes in the American South, actions undertaken with the active participation or tacit consent of entire communities. This sort of collective responsibility did not apply to the Holocaust because violent persecution of Jews (which he distinguished from anti-Semitism) was not a German folkway. Thus, "whereas anti-Negro violence in America is a real 'folk' activity, carried on against the State and its police (which, of course, wink at it), in Germany it is the reverse: pogroms are carried out by the State and the forces of 'law and order' against the folkways" (86). Exterminating Jews was a Nazi not a German folkway, and there was no evidence that the Nazis had been able through terror and propaganda to transform Germany into "one big concentration camp." Conditioning an entire population was simply not possible, and the advocates of collective responsibility who believed that the Nazis had accomplished this had confused a metaphor with a literal description.[39]

At this point in his argument, Macdonald concluded that responsibility for the Holocaust rested not with the German people but with "a particular kind of German, specialists in torture and murder, whom it would be as erroneous to confuse with the general run of Germans as it would be to confuse the brutality-specialists who form so conspicuous part of our own local police forces . . . with the average run of Americans" (85). Had he ended with this conclusion, Macdonald would have contributed little to the effort to understand the Holocaust beyond replacing a simplistic notion of collective guilt with a slightly less simplistic attribution of individual responsibility. However, the essay does not end with this conclusion. Macdonald went on to develop an argument that made "The Responsibility of Peoples" a much more interesting, complex, and important document.

Although the Nazis did not transform Germany into one big concentration camp, Macdonald observed, they did transform German society, and the Holocaust was but the most extreme and horrible manifestation of this transformation, a transformation that was at work not only in Germany but in the rest of the world as well. "Modern society," he declared, "has become so tightly organized, so rationalized and routinized that it has the character of a mechanism which grinds on without human consciousness or control. The individual, be he 'leader' or mass man, is reduced to powerlessness vis-à-vis the mechanism. More and more, things happen to people" (88). Thus, the fact that the German people were not collectively responsible for the Holocaust was not particularly good news, because their lack of responsibility resulted not from their active resistance to the Nazis but from the fact that modernity had rendered them incapable of responsible action. "If the German people are not 'responsible' for 'their' nation's war crimes," Macdonald concluded, "the world becomes a complicated and terrifying place, in which un-understood social forces move men puppetlike to perform terrible acts, and in which guilt is at once universal and meaningless. That the world is in fact such a place is quite beside the point" (88).

The death camps were the starkest evidence of this worldwide transformation. In all the reports on the camps, Macdonald noted, "the atmosphere is the same: rationality and system gone mad; the discoveries of science, the refinements of modern mass organization applied to the murder of noncombatants on a scale unknown since Genghis Khan" (84). Set up like factories, the camps produced corpses according to the soundest principles of scientific management. The Nazis had "learned much from mass production, from modern business organization" (84). Auschwitz appeared as a "sinister parody of Victorian illusions about scientific method and the desirability in itself of man's learning to control his environment" (84). The camps made human beings the objects of experimental control, stripped them of their humanity, and transformed them into things.

The processes of rationalization and the erosion of responsibility so horribly evident in the camps were at work in other realms of modern life as well. The concentration camp inmate's puppetlike behavior was, for example, mirrored in the experience of the contemporary soldier. "The modern soldier does not 'fight,'" Macdonald observed. "He 'is fought' like a battleship or other inanimate mechanism" (87). The 300 soldiers killed in the explosion of two munitions ships at Mare Island, California, in the summer of 1944 died, as most soldiers and civilians died in modern warfare, not because of any decision or action of their own but because they happened to be in the wrong place when a bomb exploded. The admiral who paid tribute to these sailors' "heroism" and "self-sacrifice" had succumbed to the instinct to "give to something which was non-purposive and impersonal a human meaning, to maintain the fiction that men who die in modern war do so not as chance victims but as active 'patriots,' who heroically choose to sacrifice their lives for their countries" (87). Sound as this instinct was, it produced "a fantastic distortion of reality" (87).

The passivity of the modern soldier was paralleled by the passivity of the modern citizen. Political responsibility, like all forms of responsibility, was proportional to the capacity to exercise it, but in politics, as elsewhere, this capacity had eroded for most. "The scale and complexity of modern governmental organization and the concentration of political power at the top are such that the vast majority of people are excluded from the participation" in decisions that shaped their lives and the lives of others (90). Without such participation, no political responsibility could be assigned, a consideration overlooked by the proponents of collective guilt. "Not for centuries," Macdonald remarked, "have individuals been at once so powerless to influence what is done by the national collectivities to which they belong, and at the same time so generally held responsible for what is done by those collectivities" (92–93).

The world, Macdonald said, has come to resemble the organic the-

ory of Nazi (and Stalinist) ideology. The modern state has become a
functionally interdependent "organism" whose parts were inseparable
from the whole. "The principles on which our mass-industry economy is built—centralization of authority, division of labor (or special-
ization of function), rigid organization from the top down into which
each worker fits at his appointed hierarchical level—these have been
carried over into the political sphere. The result is that the individual
has little choice about his behavior; and can be made to function, by
the pressure and terror wielded by the masters of the Organic State in
ways quite opposed to any he would voluntarily choose" (91).

The dialectics of this process, Macdonald said, were "wonderfully
illuminated" in a document he borrowed from an article by Arendt,
an interview by an American correspondent with a death camp official captured by the Russians:

Q. Did you kill people in the camp?

A. Yes.

Q. Did you poison them with gas?

A. Yes.

Q. Did you bury them alive?

A. It sometimes happened.

Q. Did you personally help to kill people?

A. Absolutely not. I was only the paymaster in the camp.

Q. What did you think of what was going on?

A. It was bad at first, but we got used to it.

Q. Do you know the Russians will hang you?

A. [*bursting into tears*] Why should they? What have I done? (90)

Such testimony, Macdonald argued, suggested that "it is not the
lawbreaker we must fear today so much as he who obeys the law. . . .

Only those who are willing to resist authority themselves when it conflicts too intolerably with their personal moral code, only they have the right to condemn the death-camp paymaster." Such people, he said, are few and far between. Certainly the United States could not claim to have an over-abundant supply of such people. Therefore, Macdonald asked, "Can even we really condemn the paymaster?" (91).

Resistance to rationalization and "massification" processes, Macdonald concluded, must rest less in class struggle than in exemplary acts of moral courage. The traditional defender of the common man, the labor movement, had been fully integrated into the world's various organic states and had "lost touch with the humane and democratic ideals it once believed in" (93). Relieving impotence and restoring the responsibility of peoples, he declared, required that "we must look more widely and deeply . . . to our essential humanity and to a more sensitive and passionate respect for our own and other people's humanity" (93).

A World without Responsibility

"The Responsibility of Peoples" effectively demolished the prevailing notions of the collective guilt of the German people for the Nazis' crimes, but the essay was not without its own difficulties. Chief among these was the ambiguity created by Macdonald's failure to clearly state the degree to which he believed the conditions for the exercise of moral responsibility had eroded in modern societies. This ambiguity not only rendered his call for moral resistance problematic but also limited his insight into the dynamics of the Nazis' rationalization and bureaucratization of mass murder. On the one hand, Macdonald seemed to be saying that the process of massification was far advanced, even that it had crystallized ("the world is in fact such a place"). If so, this situation entailed troubling moral consequences to which he appeared oblivious. In absolving the German people of responsibility for the Holocaust, Macdonald appeared in parts of his essay to picture a world where the conditions of responsible action had eroded to such an extent that only a few extraordinary individuals could be held responsible for their actions. In his most extreme formulations of this description ("the individual, be he 'leader' or mass-man, is reduced to powerlessness vis-à-vis the mechanism"), it was unclear not only how one could condemn the paymaster but even how one could condemn Hitler (the "leader").

Even if we pass over these extreme formulations, Macdonald still seemed to offer a view of a modern world where only the "masters of the Organic State" and the rare resister were capable of responsible (good or evil) action, while everybody else simply functioned, as one bomber pilot put it, as "a cog in one hell of a big machine" (87). In such a world, even crimes surpassing those of the paymaster were beyond responsibility. In attacking the theory of collective guilt, a theory which led to the conclusion that because everyone is guilty, no one is guilty, Macdonald had described a world in which, because virtually no one was capable of responsible action, virtually no one was guilty. Macdonald could have been read (and evidently was read by some) as replacing the theory of collective guilt with a theory of near-universal irresponsibility.[40]

Elsewhere in his essay, Macdonald qualified and muddied this dark vision. He described the increasing passivity of the modern populations as a process not yet crystallized, and he was somewhat more optimistic about the possibilities for resistance in the United States than elsewhere. "One of the most hopeful auguries for the future of this country, with the Permanent War Economy taking shape," he noted, "is that we Americans have a long and honorable tradition of lawlessness and disrespect for authority" (90). Such observations rendered Macdonald's description of the moral universe at the end of war perplexing rather than simply distressing.

The ambiguity in the essay stems principally, I think, from what might be called (to borrow Arendt's term) the rhetorical style deriving from the politics of fearful anticipation. Using descriptive language in the present tense to convey a sharper prophetic warning, Macdonald could appear to be saying that the mass society whose arrival he foresaw and feared had already arrived. Such language lent great force to his prose but did so at the risk of the very confusion of metaphor and literal description he had himself cautioned against. It also threatened Macdonald's political hope, for his concluding call for moral community and resistance appears poignant, wistful, confusing, and absurd unless we understand the cautionary thrust of his descriptive analysis.

Macdonald sensed these difficulties, and he responded quickly to readers' comments and criticisms to forestall an unduly pessimistic and morally disturbing reading of his essay. His success was mixed. In reply to one reader's criticisms, he remarked that

> On reflection, I think my article stressed the "no" too strongly, gave too much the impression that the German people have no responsibility of any kind for Nazis. This was because the problem I was dealing with was that of moral responsibility, with the consequent idea of punishment; in that sphere, responsibility can only be an individual matter, and is also related closely the individual's freedom of action. But the German people have a political responsibility for Nazism, both in that they permitted Hitler to come to power, and in that they endured his rule without revolt. For to absolve the German people of this kind of responsibility is to regard them simply as victims, dupes, or slaves, with a slavish irresponsibility.[41]

This comment clarified some of the misconceptions latent in Macdonald's rhetoric, but it raised new problems as well, as readers Jim Cork and "Louis Clair" (Lewis Coser) observed. Macdonald's attribution of collective political responsibility to the German people suffered from the same deficiencies as the "collective guilt" thesis he had attacked. Some of the German people may well bear political responsibility for the Nazis, Cork said, but certainly not all. "One section of the population was completely responsible for the advent of fascism, some partly responsible and others not at all. Neither historical fact nor moral justice warrants seeking to fasten the sense of guilt on the whole German people." Clair hinted that Macdonald's own compelling analysis of the erosion of the conditions for responsible democratic politics suggested problems for any effort to impute political responsibility to the German public. This was a telling point, but unfortunately, Macdonald did not address it.[42]

Shifting the discussion from issues of moral responsibility to those of political responsibility also moved Macdonald away from a crucial problem he had neglected in the story of the death-camp paymaster: the failure, as Reinhold Niebuhr put it, do "full justice to the infinite varieties and degrees of complicity in a group evil."[43] In identifying those responsible for the Holocaust as a select group of "specialists in torture and murder," Macdonald centered on those Nazis who had actually murdered or ordered the murder of their victims and slighted the role of the "desk murderers" who had functioned as part of the machinery of administrative massacre yet who killed no one and took no policy initiative of their own. He thus missed one of Arendt's key arguments in her article, "Organized Guilt and Universal Responsibility," from which he drew the paymaster's story. Unlike Macdonald, Arendt had begun constructing a typology of Nazi criminals that devoted particular attention to the role of "job-holders and good family-men." The Nazi leadership, she noted, knew well how to use such men as the paymaster:

> It became clear that for the sake of his pension, his life insurance, the security of his wife and children, such a man was ready to sacrifice his beliefs, his honor, and his human dignity. It needed only the satanic genius of Himmler to discover that after such degradation he was entirely prepared to do literally anything when the ante was raised and the bare existence of his family was threatened. The only condition he put was that he should be fully exempted from responsibility for his acts.[44]

Macdonald not only slighted the issues raised by Nazi desk murderers but also, ironically, outlined the terms they would use to defend themselves when charged with war crimes. Although he perceived that "it is not the lawbreaker we must fear today so much as he who obeys the law," Macdonald's description of modern society as one where "the individual has little choice about his behavior" left ambiguous his moral judgment of the law-abiding citizen. More particularly, because he did not say to what extent the conditions for exercising moral responsibility had eroded in Germany and whether Nazi desk murderers and functionaries like the death-camp paymaster could be held accountable for their actions, Macdonald unwittingly provided all the historical and sociological components for the "cog in a machine" argument Nazi organization men like Eichmann would later advanced in their own defense. As Harold Rosenberg observed during the Eichmann trial:

> The Nazi mind is nothing if not "modern"; the strength of Hitler's movement lay in its keenness regarding the perversities of present-day

experience and its cynicism in making use of them. Chief among these perversities is the sense of loss of self and responsibility that comes from functioning in a large organization. Eichmann's defense was designed to appeal to the universal appreciation of the plight of the organization man. . . . Eichmann's weeks on the stand had the effect not of breaking him down but of breaking down in the mind of the world audience the outlines, traced with such difficulty, of the Final Solution as a conspiracy of murderous men, and transforming it into an *impersonal process*.[45]

Years later, in 1962, Macdonald admitted that he needed to correct his emphasis on the deterioration of moral responsibility. "Another truth now needs to be stated," he said. "I agree that individuals are responsible for their actions and that it is disgusting when an Eichmann says 'my guilt lies in my obedience.' . . . That peoples are not responsible doesn't mean that nobody (except Hitler or Truman) is responsible." This truth needed to be stated in the forties as well.[46]

Later in 1945, Macdonald republished "The Responsibility of Peoples" as a pamphlet and included a new concluding section titled "The Community of Those Who Endure." He apparently intended this addendum to amplify his hope that responsible moral community would be revived, which he had expressed in the original essay's closing sentences. Macdonald called on the world's common people to build upon the solidarity they shared as victims and survivors, urging them to reconstruct the conditions of responsible human united action against the "Leaders" who would divide them.

When will those who endure, as soldiers or civilians, the wretchedness and filth and hunger and terror grow weary of bearing the weight of so much meaningless suffering? When will they progress from a Community of Those Who Endure to a Community of Those Who Will No

Longer Endure? When that day comes—*dies irae, dies illa!*—the Responsibility of Peoples will shift from the passive to the active mood, and they will have something really to be responsible for; no doubt terrible actions often enough, but their own and for their ends.[47]

The effect of this new section was less to raise hope—the solidarity of victimization was in and of itself a weak foundation for radical politics—than to heighten the tension in the essay between Macdonald's normative vision of humane, responsible resistance to dehumanizing evil and his deeply pessimistic vision of a modern society that was obliterating the very conditions of such resistance. It was this tension that gave "The Responsibility of Peoples" its power, and the new conclusion helped to curb the tendency for Macdonald's metaphors of rationalization to simply devour his call for moral courage. In heightening this tension, the new conclusion also highlighted the essay's strengths as a piece of ethical analysis. If "The Responsibility of Peoples" failed to provide the discriminating calculus of responsibility that the Nazis' crimes demanded, it did succeed in making a strong case for conjoining the moral and the historical imagination. Macdonald had demonstrated clearly that after the Holocaust the conventional terms of moral discourse such as "responsibility" had to be radically recalibrated to account for the altered conditions of human action in a new and frightening social world where "more and more, things happento people." Even the limitations of his argument were instructive in this respect; his ambiguity about how far this process had extended could itself serve as a spur to analysis and action.

For a time it did so for Macdonald himself. The problems he posed in "The Responsibility of Peoples" and the tension between his hopes for a revival of responsibility and his dark view of the world's tendencies would remain the hallmark of his work throughout the forties. It would shape his response to the atomic bomb, to the cold war, to the collapse of the American left, and to his own role as a radical intellectual. Yet he found the tension increasingly difficult to sustain, and the signs of its dissolution apparent in "The Responsibility of Peoples" became more and more manifest as the decade progressed. Eventually Macdonald's pessimism about the way things were overcame and shattered his dreams of the way things might be. In 1949 his money and his political hope ran out at the same time. He ceased publishing *Politics* and stopped writing about politics. Consequently, as Arendt told him, American political culture lost one of the few intellectuals with "aptitude for analysis and instinct for what is important and what is irrelevant."[48]

Legacy

When facing the Holocaust, Irving Howe said, "the beginning of moral wisdom was to admit one's intellectual bewilderment, to acknowledge we were witnessing a sharp break in the line of history. And that readiness could not come easily: our minds had been formed in the pre-Holocaust era and, strong or weak, they were the only minds we had. . . . The Holocaust had 'extended' the nature and meaning of Western history; we therefore had to reconsider man's nature, possibilities, and limits within that history."[49]

It is some measure of Dwight Macdonald's importance in American cultural history that he was among the few who were ready in 1945 to reconsider the conventional wisdom of radical politics after the disasters of World War II. That his analysis was not without its ambiguities and shortcomings is in the end less significant than that he raised the questions he did when he did. In annulling the Marxist marriage of Hope and History and wedding ethical ideals to a contingent (and potentially catastrophic) history, Macdonald not only wrote one of the most powerful reflections on the Holocaust by an American intellectual but also signaled a new era in radical social thought. The sensibility the "radical pessimism" that informed his work has remained very much a part of intellectual life after 1949. We can, for example, see it clearly at work in the thinking of such exemplary American figures as C. Wright Mills, Herbert Marcuse, Robert Heilbroner, and Christopher Lasch, and in the great English historian E. P. Thompson's jeremiads on the nuclear Holocaust that threatens us all. Macdonald's "Responsibility of Peoples" is one of those historical documents that is of more than historical interest. It stands as a virtual prologue to the crisis of moral imagination and the politics of fearful anticipation during our own time—an age after Auschwitz.

Notes

INTRODUCTION

1. *John Dewey and American Democracy* (Ithaca, NY: Cornell University Press, 1991).

2. I will not attempt to cite the considerable literature of methodological dispute produced by these two interdisciplinary efforts, but for starters see Lynn Hunt, ed., *The New Cultural History* (Berkeley: University of California Press, 1989); and H. Aram Vesser, ed., *The New Historicism* (New York: Routledge, 1989); and two essays by Jean-Christophe Agnew worrying over the consequences of each of these enterprises: "History and Anthropology: Scenes from a Marriage," *Yale Journal of Criticism* 3 (1990): 29–50, and "History and Literature: The Family Romance," manuscript.

3. Clifford Geertz, "Found in Translation: On the Social History of the Moral Imagination," in Geertz, *Local Knowledge* (New York Basic Books, 1983), 36–54. To my mind, among contemporary American historians Haskell is the best social historian of the moral imagination; see his penetrating essays in *Objectivity Is Not Neutrality: Explanatory Schemes in History* (Baltimore, Md.: Johns Hopkins University Press, 1998). The book that has had the greatest impact on my thinking about how to do the social history of the moral imagination in wartime is Michael Walzer's *Just and Unjust Wars: A Moral Argument with Historical Illustrations* (New York: Basic Books, 1977).

4. Michael Walzer, *Obligations* (Cambridge: Harvard University Press, 1970).

5. Michael Sandel, "The Political Philosophy of Contemporary Liberalism," paper delivered at the University of Rochester, 8 April 1987, 2. Sandel practices well what he preaches. See his *Democracy's Discontent: America in Search of a Public Philosophy* (Cambridge: Harvard University Press, 1996).

6. Elizabeth Anderson, "Pragmatism, Science, and Moral Inquiry," in Richard Wightman Fox and Robert B. Westbrook, eds., *In Face of the Facts: Moral Inquiry in American Scholarship* (Cambridge: Cambridge University Press, 1998), 16. The introduction that Richard Fox and I wrote for this volume further elaborates the pragmatist approach to moral inquiry I advance in this book.

7. Ibid., 15.

8. Robert Orsi, "Snakes Alive: Resituating the Moral in the Study of Religion," in Fox and Westbrook, *Face of the Facts*, 220, 223. For Orsi's own practice of this difficult art of moral inquiry at the boundary, see *The Madonna of 115th Street: Faith and Community in Italian Harlem, 1880–1950* (New Haven, Conn.: Yale University Press, 1985), and *Thank You, St. Jude: Women's Devotion to the Patron Saint of Hopeless Causes* (New Haven, Conn.: Yale University Press, 1996).

9. On the production of propaganda in World War II, see Alan M. Winkler, *The Politics of Propaganda: The Office of War Information, 1942–1945* (New Haven, Conn.: Yale University Press, 1978); John M. Blum, *V Was for Victory: Politics and American Culture during World War II* (New York: Harcourt, Brace, Jovanovich, 1976); Clayton Koppes and Gregory Black, *Hollywood Goes to War* (New York: Free Press, 1987); and Gerd Horten, *Radio Goes to War: The Cultural Politics of Propaganda during World War II* (Berkeley: University of California Press, 2003).

10. Dwight Macdonald, "The Responsibility of Peoples," *Politics* 2 (March 1945): 86–87.

11. Ibid., 88, 92–93. On Macdonald's response to terror bombing, see Robert B. Westbrook, "Horrors—Theirs and Ours: The *Politics* Circle and the Good War," *Radical History Review* 36 (1986): 9–25.

12. Daniel Bell, *The End of Ideology* (New York: Free Press, 1962), 307.

13. Macdonald, "Responsibility of Peoples," 88.

CHAPTER 1. IN THE MIRROR OF THE ENEMY

1. Michael Sandel. "Political Philosophy of Contemporary Liberalism," 2.

2. The Vietnamese might have provided a comparable challenge during the Vietnam War had Americans seen them, in the first instance, as Vietnamese rather than Communist.

3. "The Japanese," *Fortune*, February 1942, 52, 53.

4. Samuel P. Huntington, *American Politics: The Promise of Disharmony* (Cambridge: Harvard University Press, 1981), 14, 23. See also Liah Greenfeld, *Nationalism: Five Roads to Modernity* (Cambridge: Harvard University Press. 1992).

5. A solid overview of the debates concerning political obligation is John Horton, *Political Obligation* (Atlantic Highlands, NJ: Humanities Press, 1992). On liberalism's difficulties with political obligation, see Carole Pateman, *The Problem of Political*

Obligation: A Critical Analysis of Liberal Theory (Berkeley: University of California Press, 1985); A. John Simmons, *Moral Principles and Political Obligations* (Princeton, N.J.: Princeton University Press, 1979); and Michael Walter, *Obligations* (Cambridge: Harvard University Press, 1970). Other treatments of political obligation friendlier to liberalism include Philip Abbott, *The Shotgun Behind the Door: Liberalism and the Problem of Political Obligation* (Athens: University of Georgia Press, 1976); Harry Beran, *The Consent Theory of Political Obligation* (London: Croom Helm, 1987); Steven M. DeLue, *Political Obligation in a Liberal State* (Albany: SUNY Press, 1989); Richard Flathman, *Political Obligation* (New York: Atherton, 1972); George Klosko, *The Principle of Fairness and Political Obligation* (Lanham, Md.: Rowman and Littlefield, 1992); J. Roland Pennock and John W. Chapman, eds., *Political and Legal Obligation* (New York: Atherton, 1970). For a forceful defense of liberal nationalism, see Yael Tamir, *Liberal Nationalism* (Princeton, NJ: Princeton University Press, 1993).

6. Rogers Smith, "The 'American Creed' and American Identity: The Limits of Liberal Citizenship in the United States," *Western Political Quarterly* 41 (1988): 225–51; "One United People: Second-Class Female Citizenship and the American Quest for Community," *Yale Journal of Law and the Humanities* 1 (1989): 229–93; and "Beyond Tocqueville, Myrdal, and Hartz: The Multiple Traditions in America," *American Political Science Review* 87 (1993): 549–66.

7. "The Way of the Gods," *Fortune*, April 1944, 123.

8. Willard Price, "Unknown Japan," *National Geographic*, August 1942, 244; *Fortune*, "Way of the Gods," 125. On Capra's film, see William J, Blakefield, "A War Within: The Making of *Know Your Enemy—Japan*," *Sight and Sound* 52 (1983): 128–33.

9. Gustav Eckstein, "The Japanese Mind Is a Dark Corner," *Harpers,* November 1942, 665; Hugh Byas, "The Japanese Problem," *Yale Review* 32 (1942–1943): 456. See also Joseph C. Grew, *Report from Tokyo* (New York: Simon and Schuster, 1942), 14.

10. "Way of the Gods," 128; Byas, "Japanese Problem," 456; Jesse F. Steiner, *Behind the Japanese Mask* (New York: Macmillan, 1943), 105–6; William Henry Chamberlain, "Who Are These Japanese?" *American Mercury* 54 (February 1942): 157; *Guide to Japan*, CINPAC-CINCPOA Bulletin No. 209–245, 1 September 1945, 42.

11. "Half Gods After the War," *Christian Century,* 9 December 1942, 1520. See also "The Control of H. Fujino," *Fortune*, April 1944, 155–59, an effective parable about the complicity of a skeptical Japanese businessman in nationalist ideology. For a meticulous account of the Meiji invention of the imperial tradition, see Carol Gluck, *Japan's Modern Myths: Ideology in the Late Meiji Period* (Princeton, NJ: Princeton University Press, 1985). On invented traditions generally, see Eric Hobsbawm and Terence Ranger, eds., *The Invention of Tradition* (Cambridge: Cambridge University Press, 1983).

12. Chamberlain, "Who Are These Japanese?" 159. See also Carol Bache, *Paradox*

Isle (New York: Knopf, 1943), 122; Hugh Byas, *Government by Assassination* (New York: Knopf, 1942), 295–325; and Willard Price, *Japan and the Son of Heaven* (New York: Duell, Sloan and Pearce, 1945).

13. Chamberlain, "Who Are These Japanese?" 160.

14. U.S. War Department, Military Intelligence Training Center, Camp Ritchie, Maryland, *Orientation for the Pacific Theatre* (typescript, 1944), 21, copy in the World War II Collection, Manuscripts and Archives, Yale University.

15. Gustav Eckstein, "The Center of Japanese Power," *Harpers,* April 1943, 509, and "Japanese Mind Is a Dark Corner," 665.

16. Robert Sherrod, "Perhaps He Is Human," *Time,* 5 July 1943, 28–29; Mark J, Gayn, "Japan's Fanatics in Uniform," *Science Digest,* March 1942, 10–14; Hallett E. Abend, "Japan's Soldiers: Unsoldierly Yet Fanatic," *New York Times Magazine,* 11 January 1942, 12; Mark J. Gayn, "Japan Digs in to Die," *Saturday Evening Post,* 28 October 1944, 9–10; William L. Worden, "Must We Butcher Them All?" *Saturday Evening Post,* 9 December 1944, 26; and Herman Kogan, "These Nips Are Nuts," *American Magazine,* February 1945, 33.

17. Sherrod, "Perhaps He Is Human," 28.

18. "Portrait of a Japanese," *Time,* 12 January 1942, 18. See also John Goette, *Japan Fights for Asia* (New York: Harcourt, Brace, 1943), 36–51; "Jap Lieutenant: Picture Diary of His Life," *Life,* 19 June 1944, 47–48; "How Japs Fight," *Time,* 15 February 1943, 24–26; Robert Sherrod, "Nature of the Enemy," *Time,* 7 August 1944, 33; W. J. Clear, "Close-up of the Jap Fighting Man," *Reader's Digest,* November 1942, 124–30; William Munday, "Diary of a Dead Jap," *Collier's,* 25 July 1942, 5; "Jap Soldier: Range of Japanese Military Psychology," *Newsweek,* 9 November 1942, 19–21; and "Life and Death of a Jap Soldier," *Science Digest,* February 1945, 75–79.

19. Hugh Byas, *The Japanese Enemy* (New York: Knopf, 1942), vii–viii. The beehive metaphor was one of Ambassador Grew's favorites as well. See "The Future of Hirohito: Why Emperor Is Spared," *United States News,* 6 April 1945, 20. The best treatment of the Pacific war as a race war is John Dower, *War without Mercy: Race and Power in the Pacific War* (New York: Pantheon, 1986).

20. For an article based on Gorer's research, see "Why Are Japs Japs?" *Time,* 7 August 1944, 66. Ruth Benedict's treatment of Japanese character was more complex and subtle than Gorer's and others who received wider publicity during the war. Her *Chrysanthemum and the Sword* (Boston: Houghton Mifflin, 1946), based on her wartime research but not published until after the war, quickly became the most influential American study of Japanese character and culture. But as Richard Minear has argued, even Benedict was guilty of a largely ahistorical treatment of Japanese culture. See Richard H. Minear, "The Wartime Studies of Japanese National Character," *Japan Interpreter* 13 (Summer 1980): 36–59.

21. Douglas Gilbert Haring, *Blood on the Rising Sun* (Philadelphia: Macrae, Smith, 1943), 68; Joseph Newman, *Goodbye Japan* (New York: L. B. Fischer, 1942), 37.

22. Haring, *Blood on the Rising Sun*, 70; *Guide to Japan*, 32, 33; Helen Mears, "Japan's 'Divine' Mission," *Nation's Business*, December 1942, 20–21. During World War I, some prominent American intellectuals argued that Germany also had combined modern industrialism with a premodern ideology; see John Dewey, *German Philosophy and Politics* (New York: Holt, 1915); and Thorstein Veblen, *Imperial Germany and the Industrial Revolution* (New York: Macmillan, 1915).

23. *Guide to Japan*, 33.

24. "The Japanese," 56–57; *Guide to Japan*, 44–45; Nathaniel Peffer, "Fatalism—Their Strength, Their Weakness," *New York Times Magazine*, 14 December 1941, 7.

25. Byas, *Government by Assassination*, 266. Otto Tolischus appended a translation of the entire *The Way of the Subject* to his book on Japan; see Tolischus, *Tokyo Record* (New York: Reynal and Hitchcock, 1943), 405–27.

26. Dower, *War Without Mercy*, 30.

27. Ibid., 31.

28. In addition to the two following chapters, see Charles F. McGovern, "Selling the American Way: Democracy, Advertisers, and Consumers in World War II," paper delivered at the National Museum of American History, Smithsonian Institution, Washington, DC, 23 June 1987.

29 "The Japanese," 169, 168. See also Gustav Eckstein, *In Peace Japan Breeds War* (New York: Harper, 1943), 132.

30. "The Japanese," 169.

31. Karl Löwith, "The Japanese Mind," *Fortune*, December 1943, 242; Price, "Unknown Japan," 244.

32. *Guide to Japan*, 3. See also Byas, *Japanese Enemy*, 37.

33. "Portrait of a Japanese," 18.

34. See chapter two.

35. Löwith "Japanese Mind," 240.

36. Löwith, "Japanese Mind," 241. I have borrowed the terms "family state" and "state of families" from Amy Gutmann, *Democratic Education* (Princeton, NJ: Princeton University Press, 1987), 22–33.

37. Löwith "Japanese Mind," 240.

38. Willis Lamott, *Nippon: The Crime and Punishment of Japan* (New York: John Day, 1944), 8; Otto Tolischus, "The Savage Code that Rules Japan," *New York Times Magazine*, 6 February 1944, 37.

39. Emmet Lavery, "The Enemy in Perspective," *Commonweal*, 19 November 1943, 114; Tolischus, "Savage Code," 36.

40. General Electric, "This Fight Is a Family Affair," *Life*, 24 August 1942, 14–15. I

had intended to reproduce this ad, but I was denied permission by a GE representative who was worried that a reference in it to the bombing of Pearl Harbor by the "Japs" would offend the Japanese, with whom, I was assured, GE now has a very congenial relationship. For a discussion of some graphic representations of an American family state headed by Uncle Sam, see chapter two.

41. See my discussion of Norman Rockwell's painting, *Freedom of Speech*, in chapter two.

42. For a full sampling of appeals to racial solidarity, see Dower, *War Without Mercy*, 77–200. On racial arguments for internment and liberal arguments against it, see Peter Irons, *Justice at War* (New York: Oxford, 1983).

43. Such a thicker liberal nationalism might, for example, be said to characterize the "antifoundational," historicist, and benignly "ethnocentrist" liberalism of philosopher Richard Rorty; see *Contingency, Irony, and Solidarity* (Cambridge: Cambridge University Press, 1989), 44–69, 189–98; *Objectivity, Relativism, and Truth: Philosophical Papers* (Cambridge: Cambridge University Press, 1991), 175–210; and "The Unpatriotic Academy," *New York Times*, 13 February 1994, 15.

CHAPTER 2. FIGHTING FOR THE AMERICAN FAMILY

1. Carole Pateman, *The Problem of Political Obligation: A Critique of Liberal Theory* (Berkeley: University of California Press, 1985). 1.

2. See A. John Simmons, *Moral Principles and Political Obligations* (Princeton, NJ: Princeton University Press, 1979); and Michael Walzer, *Obligations* (Cambridge: Harvard University Press, 1970). Pateman's *Problem of Political Obligation* might be said to blast liberalism with both barrels.

3. Walzer, *Obligations*, 82.

4. Ibid.

5. Walzer, *Obligations*, 89, 205–207.

6. Ibid., 89.

7. Norman Rockwell, *Norman Rockwell: My Adventures as an Illustrator* (Garden City, NY: Doubleday, 1960), 338.

8. Ibid., 338–39.

9. Ibid., 343.

10. Stephen Vincent Benet, "Freedom from Fear," *Saturday Evening Post*, 13 March 1943, 12.

11. Norman Rockwell, "Freedom from Want," *Saturday Evening Post*, 6 March 1943, 13; Rockwell, *Norman Rockwell*, 343. (Rockwell reported that many Europeans resented this painting "because it wasn't freedom from want, it was overabundance, the table was so loaded down with food.") "Freedom from want" was the most controversial of the war aims proclaimed by Roosevelt because it obliged the liberal state

to provide and protect a minimal level of subsistence for the individuals it comprises. This obviously is not conveyed to Rockwell's painting, but it is something that Benet appears to have worried over on behalf of more traditional liberals in his essay on fear, in which he emphasized that "freedom from fear" did not mean "freedom from struggle and toil, from hardship and danger. We do not intend to breed a race wrapped in cotton wool, too delicate to stand rough weather"; see Benet, "Freedom from Fear," 12. On the other hand, the *Post* essay titled "Freedom from Want" by Carlos Bulosan, a Philippine immigrant who had suffered a good deal of rough weather in the thirties as a labor organizer, articulated the position of the welfare-state liberal and stood in curious contrast with Rockwell's illustration on the facing page as well as, it should be said, with Roosevelt's implicit contention that freedom from want was something that the New Deal had secured for Americans who now wished to extend it to the rest of the world. Speaking on behalf of those in America who are "not really free" because they have not been granted freedom from want and who wonder "if we are really a part of America," Bulosan advanced what might be termed the "immanent" critique of a liberal theory of political obligation grounded in the receipt of benefits from the state; see Bulosan, "Freedom from Want," *Saturday Evening Post*, 6 March 1943, 12. This critique was most forcefully argued during the war by some black Americans, who contended that, if citizens were obligated to defend the state because of the benefits they received from it, then they were less obliged than others to defend the American state because it provided them with fewer benefits than it did other citizens.

12. United States Rubber Company, "What Are We Fighting For?" *Life,* 12 October 1942, 63.

13. Union Central Life Insurance Company, "War and the Family Man," *Life,* 23 February 1942, 73.

14. Western Electric, "More Aluminum Up There, Less in New Telephones—for Victory!" *Life,* 23 February 1942, 41.

15. "Mother She Keeps Home Warm for Her Sons When They Go Off to War," *Life,* 28 December 1942, 59–62. On Betty Grable and other pin-ups, see chapter three.

16. Union Central Life Insurance Company, "The Person Named Herein Has Been Classified 3A," *Life,* 23 March 1942, 5; Eureka Vacuum Cleaners, "My Heart's Overseas but My Hands Are on the Job," *Saturday Evening Post,* 21 August 1943, 81.

17. W&J Sloane, "I'm Too Old to Dream," *New Yorker,* 14 October 1944, 5. See also Charles F. McGovern, "Selling the American Way Democracy, Advertisers, and Consumers in World War II," paper delivered at the National Museum of American History, Smithsonian Institution, 1987.

18. My arguments are also borne out by research on contemporary American attitudes about citizenship. See Pamela J. Conover, Ivor M. Crewe, and Donald P. Searing,

"The Nature of Citizenship in the United States and Great Britain: Empirical Comments on Theoretical Themes," *Journal of Politics* 53 (1991): 800–32.

19. Amy Gutmann, *Democratic Education* (Princeton, NJ: Princeton University Press, 1987), 22–33; General Electric, "This Fight Is a Family Affair," *Life*, 24 August 1942, 14–15.

20. On Japanese prescriptions for political obligation see, in addition to chapter one, *Kokutai no Hongi: Cardinal Principles of the National Entity of Japan*, ed. Robert K. Hall (Cambridge: Harvard University Press, 1949). For a superb discussion of these prescriptions and the American response to them see John Dower, *War without Mercy: Race and Power in the Pacific War* (New York: Pantheon, 1986), 28–32, 279–85.

21. I will say nothing here about *Freedom of Worship* because it portrays a set of nonfamilial (albeit private) and nonpolitical obligations and interests.

22. Hannah Arendt, *The Human Condition* (Chicago: University of Chicago Press, 1958), 27.

23 Booth Tarkington, "Freedom of Speech," *Saturday Evening Post*, 20 February 1943, 28; Walzer, *Obligations*, 91–92.

24. Walzer, *Obligations*, 211–13.

25. Ibid.

CHAPTER 3. "I WANT A GIRL, JUST LIKE THE GIRL THAT MARRIED HARRY JAMES"

1. Maureen Dowd, "For Bush, Culture Can Be a Sometime Thing," *New York Times*, 27 October 1988, B15. Doris Day, who made her first movie in 1948, was not a World War II pin-up girl, but as the analysis that follows indicates, Bush's mistake in singling out the later Hollywood model of the "girl-next-door" as his favorite is suggestive.

2. Paul Fussell has noted the difficulties Americans had during World War II formulating a compelling answer to the question "what are we fighting for?" In the wake of World War I and the peace treaty that concluded it, wars for abstract, universal (and vague) moral principles had lost their appeal. Fussell goes on, however, to claim that Americans eventually met this uncertainty by resorting to "non-ideological" appeals such as the one in a Carnation Milk ad arguing that soldiers were fighting for their babies ("thriving on Carnation"). I contend that this sort of argument is not nonideological but one characteristic of liberal ideology, which legitimates war as the discharge of private obligations. See Fussell, *Wartime: Understanding and Behavior in the Second World War* (New York: Oxford University Press, 1989), 139.

3. I am indebted to my colleague Mary Young for recalling the parody of the popular song title that I allude to in this chapter's title, which was apparently a popular piece of wartime folklore. (I have resisted the temptation to correct its grammar.) Her

recollection is confirmed in *Time* magazine's cover story on Betty Grable ("Living the Daydream," 23 August 1948, 40). My focus here on the pin-up ignores the cultural construction of another important group of women as icons of obligation: mothers. Mothers were a very significant feature of wartime propaganda and the felt obligations of American soldiers. The general character of the obligation between men and their mothers is similar to that between men and other women (what I shall call the asymmetrical commitments of protector and protected), but the unique features of the former obligation merit an extended consideration that I cannot provide in this chapter.

4. For some further examples of rape propaganda, see "War Posters: American Artists Go All Out for Victory in Big Picture Campaign," *Life*, 21 December 1942, 54–56. The enemy was well aware of this sort of propaganda and attempted to counter it with the suggestion that, when it came to the expropriation of sexual property, the Allies posed a greater threat to one another than the Germans and the Japanese; see Susan Gubar, "'This Is My Rifle, This Is My Gun': World War II and the Blitz on Women" in *Behind the Lines Gender and the Two World Wars*, ed. Margaret R. Higonnet, Jane Jenson, Sonya Michel, and Margaret Collins Weitz (New Haven, Conn.: Yale University Press, 1987), 238–39.

5. On the history of the pin-up, see Mark Gabor, *The Pin-Up: A Modest History* (New York: Universe Books, 1972), and Ralph Stein, *The Pin-Up from 1852 to Today* (New York: Hamlyn, 1981).

6. "Seductive Irene Manning," *Yank*, 28 July 1944, 14; Paul Fussell, "*Yank* When We Needed It," in Fussell, *The Boy Scout Handbook and Other Observations* (New York: Oxford University Press, 1982), 228.

7. John D'Emilio and Estelle Freedman, *Intimate Matters: A History of Sexuality in America* (New York: Harper and Row, 1988), 274, illustration 60; Jane Gaines, "The Showgirl and the Wolf," *Cinema Journal* 20 (1980): 59, 65.

8. Fussell, "*Yank* When We Needed It," 228; "Seductive Irene Manning," 14; Ladd quoted in Jane Gaines, "The Popular Icon as Commodity and Sign: The Circulation of Betty Grable, 1941–45" (PhD diss., Northwestern University, 1982), 459–60; the editors of *Look*, *Movie Lot to Beachhead* (Garden City, NY: Double Day, 1945), 105. Differences in appeal should be observed, I think, not only between the images of different pin-up stars but also between photographic pin-ups and pin-up drawings like those of Albert Vargas, that is, between *Life* pin-ups and *Esquire* pin-ups.

9. On Grable's predominantly working-class audience, see Gaines, "Popular Icon as Commodity and Sign," 16, 293, 484–94; see also John Costello, *Virtue Under Fire: How World War II Changed Our Social and Sexual Attitudes* (Boston: Little, Brown, 1985), 149–50. Betty Grable has not been well served by her biographers. She is the subject of two decidedly inferior instances of the suspect genre of the star-bio: Doug

Warren, *Betty Grable: The Reluctant Movie Queen* (New York: St. Martins, 1981); and Spero Pastos, *Pin-Up: The Tragedy of Betty Grable* (New York: Berkeley, 1986). Grable was a very vulgar woman, but this vulgarity was repressed in her films. As James Harvey says, "She was the tough-girl type—but in the 1940s she wasn't allowed to be that, the way leading women in the 1930s had been, from Jean Harlow to Ginger Rogers. Grable's obvious vulgarity—which might have linked her to the best and strongest traditions of Hollywood comedy—became instead a touchy matter, a potential embarrassment." Avoiding this embarrassment was essential to constructing Grable as the leading pin-up; see James Harvey, "Screen Gems," *New York Review of Books*, 30 June 1988, 23.

10. Richard Schickel, *The Stars* (New York: Bonanza Books, 1962), 217; "Living the Daydream," 40; Andre Bazin, "Entomology of the Pin-Up Girl" in Bazin, *What Is Cinema?* (Berkeley: University of California Press, 1971), 2:158–162; "Betty Grable's Legs," *Life*, 7 June 1943, 82. This latter article, which features eleven photographs of a headless Grable's legs, is a superb example of the way advertising and other mass media presented women as disassembled body parts.

11. "G. I.s and Movies," *Time*, 31 July 1944, 50.

12. Gaines, "Popular Icon as Commodity and Sign," 51, 478, 502; Pastos, *Pin-Up*, 60; Schickel, *Stars*, 217; "Grable's Baby," *Life*, 8 May 1944, 32. I do not mean to imply here that Betty Grable served in any direct way to motivate participating in combat. As classic studies of men in combat such as Samuel Stouffer et al., eds., *The American Soldier* (Princeton, NJ: Princeton University Press, 1965) have shown, most soldiers were motivated to fight less by ideology than by such considerations as loyalty to their buddies (itself a private obligation) and sheer survival. Ideology, such as that analyzed in this chapter, explains more about "why we serve" or "what are we fighting for" than about "why we fight," more narrowly conceived. As psychologist John Dollard remarked, "The soldier in battle is not forever whispering, 'My cause, my cause.' He is too busy for that. Ideology functions *before* battle, to get the man in; and *after* battle by blocking thoughts of escape"; quoted in Richard Holmes, *Acts of War: The Behavior of Men in Battle* (New York: Free Press, 1985), 276. Holmes's book is an excellent discussion of these issues.

13. Costello, *Virtue Under Fire*, 154. For further examples of "nose art," see Gary Valent, *Vintage Aircraft Nose Art* (Osceola, Wis.: MBI Publishing, 1989).

14. Judith Hicks Stiehm, "The Protected, the Protector, the Defender," *Women's Studies International Forum* 5 (1982): 367–76; Gubar, "This Is My Rifle," esp. 251–55. Stiehm also argues that the protected suffers because, in the protector-protected relationship, they rely on "surrogate executioners." This distance from the slaughter "makes it easier for women to ignore, to condone, or even to support actions they would not take themselves," and it renders them more able to stereotype and dehumanize the

enemy (370). It also means that women are more likely to be poorly informed about wars and lack the skepticism that protectors have about official information.

15. These two obligations often conflicted for women who worked for the war effort. Although advertisements and other propaganda urged women simultaneously to work at a lathe while remaining a pin-up, factory managers concerned about sexual fraternization on the shop floor made this dual task difficult. The obligation that women be workers for their men is yet another important aspect of American conceptions of political obligation during the war that cannot be addressed here.

16. "Living the Daydream," 40; Gaines, "Popular Icon as Commodity and Sign," 457, 459, 465. Encouraging women to be self-effacing would be important advice to women helping soldiers adjust to civilian life, another of the important obligations urged on women during wartime; see Susan M. Hartmann, "Prescriptions for Penelope: Literature on Women's Obligations to Returning World War II Veterans," *Women's Studies* 5 (1978): 223–39.

17. "Inspiration: Girl's Photo Spurs U. S. Tank Corporal on to Valor at Oran," *Life,* 30 November 1942, 126–29. Apparently, Bernie Kessel inadvertently left Rita Weinberg's photo in his tank when it was passed on to another regiment, and she was adopted as a pin-up girl by the soldiers who inherited it. Thus her picture came to serve surrogate functions similar to Betty Grable's, though on a far less massive scale. See "Long Arm of Coincidence," *Life,* 7 June 1943, 4. Women wanting expert advice on making homemade pin-ups could find it in articles such as Roman Freulick, "Make Your Own Pinups," *Popular Photography,* September 1944,): 22–23+. I am grateful to Bruce Leslie for this reference.

18. Pete Martin, "Tonight at the Beachhead Bijou," *Saturday Evening Post,* 12 August 1944, 82.

CHAPTER 4. THE RESPONSIBILITY OF PEOPLES

1. Alfred Kazin, *Starting Out in the Thirties* (Boston: Little, Brown, 1965), 165–66; Kazin, *New York Jew* (New York: Knopf, 1978), 4, 26. Kazin's experience in a movie theater suggests the power of photographic images to overcome the skepticism that greeted reports of mass extermination earlier in the war. As Susan Sontag has observed: "photographs shock insofar as they show something novel. . . . One's first encounter with the photographic inventory of ultimate horror is a kind of revelation, the proto-typically modern revelation: a negative epiphany." At the same time, "the ethical content of photographs is fragile," and a distant horror made "more real" by photographs can after repeated exposure become less real. Sontag suggests that because photographs of the Nazi death camps have become "ethical reference points," they may be immune to this process; see Sontag, *On Photography* (New York: Farrar, Straus and Giroux, 1977), 19–20. Sontag is unduly hopeful. See Lesley Hazelton, "The

Esthetic View of Death," a review of three coffee-table books on the Holocaust, *Nation*, 21 November 1981, 529–31; and Dwight Macdonald, *On Movies* (New York: Da Capo, 1981), 447–49.

2. Kazin, *New York Jew*, 194–95.

3. Members of this group included Lionel Abel, Hannah Arendt, William Barrett, Daniel Bell, Clement Greenberg, Sidney Hook, Irving Howe, Irving Kristol, Mary McCarthy, Dwight Macdonald, William Phillips, Norman Podhoretz, Philip Rahv, Harold Rosenberg, Meyer Schapiro, Delmore Schwartz, and Lionel Trilling. As yet, no one has written an adequate historical study of this community, but see William Barrett, *The Truants* (New York: Doubleday, 1982); Irving Howe, "The New York Intellectuals," in *Decline of the New* (New York: Harcourt, Brace and World, 1970); and Stephen A. Longstaff, "The New York Family," *Queen's Quarterly*, 83 (1976): 556–73.

4. Karla Goldman, "The Abyss Was at Our Feet: The Response of the New York Intellectuals to the Destruction of European Jewry" (senior essay, Department of History, Yale University, 1982), 5. My discussion of this issue closely follows the analysis in this essay and reflects as well many fruitful conversations with its author.

5. Pearl Bell, "The Meaning of PR," *New Republic,* 17 March 1982, 32; Solomon Bloom, "The Great Unvolved Crime," *Commentary* 19 (1955): 89; Goldman, "The Abyss," 8–15.

6. "A New Theory of Totalitarianism," *New Leader* 34 (14 May 1951): 17–18.

7. See Macdonald, "What Is Totalitarianism?" *New Leader* 34 (9 July, 1951): 17n. Arendt saluted Macdonald in 1946 as

> an honest, stubborn, restless thinker . . . concerned less with creating a role for himself as a lion and pundit, and less with immaculate and impossible consistency than with really struggling with the problems that perplex our age. What I like best about Mr. Macdonald is his courageous willingness to go beyond the fashionable and orthodox unorthodoxies which constitute so great a danger for any person who is really trying to think today. . . . Macdonald has turned his back on every kind of doctrine that implicitly would treat man as an object even from a benevolent point of view. What he is concerned with is to create a modern humanism that can hold its own in the face of enormous bureaucracies and the atomic bomb. In so doing he has had to renounce many things which he had heretofore energetically championed. This is further evidence of what a really serious person he is.

Hannah Arendt to Houghton Mifflin Fellowship Committee, 24 December 1946, Dwight Macdonald Papers, Yale University.

8. I am aware of the judgments implied by my analysis. They are unavoidable and I do not mean to avoid them, only to temper them with an understanding of the cir-

cumstances in which these intellectuals found themselves. The burden of this task is relieved somewhat by Howe's invitation: "Should we be judged, then, for the slowness with which we registered the meaning of the Holocaust? Yes, and why not? Intellectuals are never slow to judge the responses of others"; see Howe, "Mid-Century Turning Point," *Midstream* 21 (1975): 25.

9. Howe, *Margin of Hope* (New York: Harcourt Brace Jovanovich, 1982), 248.

10. Lionel Trilling quoted in Howe, *Margin of Hope*, 248; Isaac Rosenfeld, "Terror Beyond Evil" (1948), in Theodore Solotaroff, ed., *An Age of Enormity* (Cleveland: World, 1962), 197.

11. Hannah Arendt, "The Concentration Camp," *Partisan Review* 15 (1948): 743–47 (this was the only substantial article on the Holocaust that *Partisan Review* published in the 1940s); Bloom, "Great Unsolved Crime," 93; Goldman, "Abyss," 33.

12. Howe, *Margin of Hope*, 249–50; Franz Neumann, *Behemoth: The Structure and Practice of National Socialism* (New York: Oxford University Press, 1942), 125. Nazism and the Holocaust have continued to present severe difficulties for Marxists. The best radical histories of the Third Reich are those of historians such as Tim Mason who have departed significantly from conventional Marxist categories of explanation; see T. W. Mason, "The Primacy of Politics: Politics and Economics in National Socialist Germany," in S. J. Woolf, ed., *The Nature of Fascism* (New York: Random House, 1969), 165–202; and Pierre Aycoberry, *The Nazi Question* (New York: Pantheon, 1981), 149–79.

13. Kazin, *New York Jew*, 44; see also David Hollinger, "Ethnic Diversity, Cosmopolitanism, and the Emergence of the American Liberal Intelligentsia," *American Quarterly* 27 (1975): 133–54.

14. "Under Forty," *Contemporary Jewish Record* 7 (1944): 15–17.

15. Elliot Cohen, "The Intellectuals and the Jewish Community," *Commentary* 8 (1949): 24.

16. Kazin, quoted in "Under Forty," 10; Goldman, "Abyss," 15–23.

17. Irving Howe to Dwight Macdonald, 14 February 1949; Howe to Macdonald, n.d. (probably February 1949), Macdonald Papers; Howe, "Magazine Chronicle," *Partisan Review* 16 (1949): 425–26; Sidney Hook, "Reflections on the Jewish Question," *Partisan Review* 16 (1949): 467.

18. William Barrett, "A Prize for Ezra Pound," *Partisan Review* 16 (1949): 344–47; W. H. Auden et al., "The Question of the Pound Award," *Partisan Review* 16 (1949): 512–22.

19. Cohen, "Intellectuals and the Jewish Community," 24; Howe, quoted in Goldman, "Abyss," 30. A related phenomenon was the careful attention New York intellectuals gave to social scientists' "generic studies" of such topics as "prejudice" and the "authoritarian personality." *Commentary*'s superb "Study of Man" series was exem-

plary in this regard. Just as it was easier to talk about the nature of totalitarian society than it was to confront the Holocaust, so too it was easier to talk about racial prejudice than to confront the death camps. The nomological ambitions of social science served to distance academics and intellectuals from the painful particulars of history.

20. Daniel Bell, "The Alphabet of Justice," *Partisan Review* 30 (1963): 418.

21. Kazin, *New York Jew*, 195.On Arendt's theory of totalitarianism, see Stephen Whitfield's penetrating study, *Into the Dark* (Philadelphia: Temple University Press, 1980).

22. Bell, "Alphabet of Justice," 428; Marie Syrkin, "Miss Arendt Surveys the Holocaust," *Jewish Frontier* 30 (May 1963): 14; Howe, *Margin of Hope*, 251. Some New York intellectuals recognized the close connection between Arendt's concept of totalitarianism and her analysis in *Eichmann in Jerusalem* and argued that both should be rejected. Norman Podhoretz, for example, suggested that "what Miss Arendt's book on the Eichmann trial teaches us about the Nature of Totalitarianism is that the time has come to re-examine the whole concept." The theory "has always been limited in its usefulness by the quasi-metaphysical and rather Germanic terms in which it was originally conceived." For Podhoretz, it was not the act but the victim that was salient, and he called for renewed attention to Nazi racism. The lessons to be learned from the Holocaust, he said, were lessons about anti-Semitism; see Podhoretz, "Hannah Arendt on Eichmann: A Study in the Perversity of Brilliance," *Commentary* 36 (1963): 206–7. For a more recent account of the *Eichmann in Jerusalem* controversy, see Elizabeth Young-Bruehl's fine biography, *Hannah Arendt* (New Haven, Conn.: Yale University Press, 1982), chapter 8; but see also Whitfleld, *Into the Dark*, chapters 6 and 7. A full discussion of the Eichmann affair would have to include an account of Arendt's complex conception of her own identity as a Jewish "pariah." See her essays in Ronald Feldman, ed., *The Jew as Pariah* (New York: Grove Press, 1978) and Leon Botstein, "Liberating the Pariah: Politics, the Jews, and Hannah Arendt," *Salmagundi* 60 (1983): 73–106.

23. Dwight Macdonald, "Hannah Arendt and the Jewish Establishment," in Macdonald, *Discriminations* (New York: Viking, 1974), 308–17.

24. Daniel Bell, "The Mood of Three Generations," in *The End of Ideology* (New York: Free Press, 1962), 307. Macdonald's discussion of the Holocaust in "The Responsibility of Peoples" was preceded by Bruno Bettelheim's "Behavior in Extreme Situations," *Politics* 1 (August 1944): 199–209. This article first appeared in the October 1943 *Journal of Abnormal and Social Psychology*, but it was its republication in *Politics* that brought it to the attention of American intellectuals. It has since then been a touchstone for discussions of dehumanization and resistance in the concentration camps. Other discussions of the Holocaust in the magazine included Macdonald,

"The Jews, *The New Leader*, and Old Judge Hull," *Politics* 2 (January 1945): 23–25; "Max Lerner and the German People," *Politics* 2 (April 1945): 102–3; "Is Thomas Mann a German?," *Politics* 2 (April 1945): 103; Jan Levcik, "Buchenwald before the War," *Politics* 2 (June 1945): 173–74; "Absolution," *Politics* 2 (July 1945): 194–95; Bruno Bettelheim, "War Trials and German Re-Education," *Politics* 2 (November 1945): 368–69; "The German Experience—Three Documents," *Politics* 3 (October 1946): 314–19; and David Rousset, "The Days of Our Death," *Politics* 4 (July-August 1947): 151–57.

25. Undated "R of P" ms. fragment, Macdonald Papers (box 74/file 93); Macdonald to Nicola Chiaromonte, 14 April 1949; Chiaromonte to Macdonald, 7 June 1949; William Phillips to Macdonald, 17 January 1949; Irving Howe to Macdonald, 8 May 1949; Macdonald to Howe, 21 May 1949, Macdonald Papers; "Semitism" (1949), unpublished ms., Macdonald Papers; "Homage to Twelve Judges," *Politics* 6 (Winter 1949): 1. Pound himself was among these critics. "My dear Macdonald," he wrote, "You are certainly one of the most ignorant apes that ever reached a typewriter & evidently void of all curiosity re historical fact. That is, I take it you lie from ignorance rather than malice" (Ezra Pound to Macdonald, 26 April 1949, Macdonald Papers).

26. Macdonald, "Hannah Arendt and the Jewish Establishment," 312, 316; Macdonald to William Phillips, 29 June 1963; Macdonald to Phillips, 16 July 1963, Macdonald Papers. In discussions with me, Macdonald dismissed the importance of ethnic conflict among the New York intellectuals; but he then proceeded to refer to Philip Rahv repeatedly as a "coarse, crude, brutish Ukrainian peasant" (Dwight Macdonald, interview by author, 4 December 1981).

27. Dwight Macdonald, "Introduction" to Macdonald, *Politics Past* (New York: Viking, 1957), 19–22; "The Root Is Man," *Politics* 3 (April, 1946): 97–115, (July 1946): 194–214; Macdonald to Dinsmore Wheeler, 26 June 1945, Macdonald Papers.

28. Dwight Macdonald, interview by author, 5 January 1982. On Macdonald's early antiwar politics and his split with *Partisan Review*, see Stephen A. Longstaff, "Partisan Review and the Second World War," *Salmagundi* 43 (1979): 108–29. "The Responsibility of Peoples" was the fifth article in the "War as an Institution" series; the others were: Macdonald, "On the Psychology of Killing" (September 1944); Bernard Lemann, "The Aesthetics of Bombing" (October 1944); Llewellyn Queener, "Inter-Enemy Ethics" (December 1944); Simone Weil, "Reflections on War" (February 1945); Ed Seldon, "Military Society" (October 1945); and Simone Weil, "Words and War" (March 1946). In his outstanding book, *Just and Unjust Wars* (New York: Basic, 1977), Michael Walzer discusses the distinction between *jus ad bellum* and *jus in bello* and the moral issues raised by each.

29. "Reaction from Europe," *Politics* 2 (September 1945): 285–86. See also "Lecture on the Refugee Problem" (1939), ms., Macdonald Papers; Macdonald, "The

Jews, *The New Leader*, and Old Judge Hull." James Wilkinson analyzes the themes of resistance thinking in his excellent book, *Intellectual Resistance in Europe* (Cambridge: Harvard University Press, 1981).

30. I am indebted to Robert Cummings for this point.

31. "The Politics of Illusion," *Partisan Review* 13 (1946): 612–14; Macdonald, "*Partisan Review* and *Politics*," *Politics* 3 (December 1946): 400–403. Macdonald told me that Philip Rahv asked him how he could edit a magazine called *Politics*: "You don't know anything about politics because you don't know anything about power." "Politics," Macdonald responded, "has to do with morality." "If that's what you think," Rahv said, "why don't you join the Catholic Church or Quakers?" (Dwight Macdonald, interview with author, 4 December, 1981). Again, the contempt of Rahv and other "realists" for ethics can be traced, in part, to the prevailing Marxist wisdom. Informing one correspondent of the tremendous response from readers to his publication of Simone Weil's essay, "The Iliad, or the Poem of Force" (November 1945), Macdonald noted that "the only people who didn't understand how such an article had a place in a political journal were—and I think this is profoundly significant—all of them Marxists. To a Marxist, an analysis of human behavior from an ethical point of view is just not 'serious'—even smacks a little of religion" (Macdonald to Art Wiser, 16 January 1946, Macdonald Papers).

32. Arendt, *Eichmann in Jerusalem*, rev. ed. (New York: Viking, 1965), 268; Young-Bruehl, *Hannah Arendt*, 201.

33. Dwight Macdonald, "The Responsibility of Peoples," *Politics* 2 (March 1945): 82 (subsequent page references to this essay appear in the text). In September 1945, Terence Donaghue criticized Macdonald in a letter to *Politics* for remarks he had made dating Allied knowledge of the Nazi death camps from the summer of 1944 and offering evidence of such knowledge as early as the beginning of 1942. "Terence Donaghue," identified as a ferret farmer from Staten Island, was the pseudonym Macdonald sometimes used when he wished to criticize his own work; he was here publicly upbraiding himself for his mistakes, as he often did.

34. Solomon Bloom and Gordon Cronan, "The Rationality of Death Camps," *Politics* 2 (July 1945): 203–4.

35. Ibid., 204.

36. Hannah Arendt "Social Science Techniques and the Study of Concentration Camps," *Jewish Social Studies* 12 (1950): 40.

37. Dwight Macdonald, "What Is Totalitarianism? (2)," *New Leader* 34 (16 July 1951): 18. Macdonald was still wrestling ambiguously with these issues in 1948; see "Death Camps and Rationality," *Politics* 5 (Summer 1948): 205. He did finally arrive at a conception of totalitarian ideology similar to Arendt's in an unpublished essay he

wrote in 1949 titled "The Dream World of the Soviet Bureaucracy" (ms. in Macdonald Papers).

38. Macdonald's focus on collective guilt was probably determined in part by the prominence of the concept in the thinking of pro-Soviet, fellow-traveling liberals such as Max Lerner, for whom Macdonald never hesitated to express his contempt. See Macdonald, "Max Lerner and the German People"; "Totalitarian Liberalism—3 Specimens," *Politics* 2 (August 1945): 254–55.

39. Cf. Bettelheim, "Behavior in Extreme Situations," 209.

40. See, for example, "Letter from a Sergeant," *Politics* 2 (May 1945): 132, where the writer complimented Macdonald on his essay and applied his interpretation of the piece to his own experience investigating a "horror hospital" in Germany. "In modern society there is evil but there is no devil. Murder has been mechanized and rendered impersonal. The foul deed of bloody hands belongs to a bygone era when man could commit his own sins. Now innocence or guilt is a problem beyond the scope of court and legal decision. Here, as in many other cases, the guilt belonged to the machine. Somewhere in the apparatus of bureaucracy, memoranda, and clean efficient directives, a crime had been committed. Men died in a hospital, of starvation, of medical neglect. But the witnesses were very 'unsatisfactory'—who was responsible, the [Inspector General] would never discover. *What* was responsible could, I think, be established, and convicted, but I am afraid the old man is searching for a 'suspect' he can sit down in the witness chair and ply with the routine of cross examination. The chair will remain empty. and the crimes will go on."

41. Exchange with Guenter Reimann, in a follow-up essay, "The Responsibility of Peoples," *Politics* 2 (May 1945): 155.

42. "Moral vs. Political Responsibility," *Politics* 2 (July 1945): 206–9.

43. Reinhold Niebuhr, "The 'Responsibility of Peoples,'" *Politics* 2 (May 1945), 160.

44. Arendt, "Organized Guilt and Universal Responsibility," in *The Jew as Pariah*, 232. Arendt later developed this insight, in her Eichmann book, into a conception of the "banality of evil." This notion drew a great deal of criticism, but most of it focused on the applicability of the idea to Eichmann, not to the idea itself. Christopher Browning has demonstrated the concept's utility for understanding the actions of an important group of middle-level bureaucrats in the murder machinery; see Browning, *Final Solution and the German Foreign Office: A Study of Referat DSIII of Abteilung Deutschland, 1940–1943* (New York: Holmes and Meier, 1978).

45. Harold Rosenberg, "The Trial and Eichmann," *Commentary* 32 (1961): 379–80, 381; Macdonald to Gordon Zahn, 22 May 1962, Macdonald Papers. Macdonald's letter was in response to Zahn's "The Private Conscience and Legitimate Authority," *Commonweal* 76 (30 March 1962): 9–13.

46. Dwight Macdonald, "The Private Conscience," *Commonweal* 76 (6 July 1962): 378.

47. Dwight Macdonald, *The Responsibility of Peoples* (New York: *Politics* Pamphlet, 1945), 16.

48. Hannah Arendt to Macdonald, 16 August 1951, Macdonald Papers. Macdonald's increasing pessimism became apparent when subsequent reprintings of "The Responsibility of Peoples" dropped the new conclusion to the 1945 pamphlet version. A superb analysis of the dynamics of Macdonald's thinking during the postwar period is Robert Cummings, "Resistance and Victimization: Dwight Macdonald as a Critical Thinker in the 1940s," paper presented at the Pacific Coast Branch of the American Historical Association, San Francisco, 1978. It should be noted that Macdonald returned to political activism and writing in the 1960s as a vigorous opponent of the war in Vietnam; see Norman Mailer, *Armies of the Night* (New York: New American Library, 1968), 37–38.

49. Howe, *Margin of Hope*, 250.

Bibliographical Note

I have made no effort to update the endnotes, but I will append a modest bibliographical note directing interested readers to some of the literature I have found illuminating that has been published since these essays first appeared.

The volume in which the first chapter appeared, John Bodnar, ed., *Bonds of Affection: Americans Define Their Patriotism* (Princeton, NJ: Princeton University Press, 1996), contains several other instructive essays on the peculiarities of American patriotism. Rogers Smith has contributed two especially stimulating books to debates over American national identity: *Civic Ideals: Conflicting Visions of Citizenship in U.S. History* (New Haven, Conn.: Yale University Press, 1997); and *Stories of Peoplehood: The Politics and Morals of Political Membership* (Cambridge: Cambridge University Press, 2003). See also John Bodnar, *Remaking America: Public Memory, Commemoration, and Patriotism in the Twentieth Century* (Princeton, NJ: Princeton University Press, 1992); Jonathan Hansen, *The Lost Promise of Patriotism: Debating American Identity, 1890–1920* (Chicago: University of Chicago Press, 2003); and Cecilia O'Leary, *To Die For: The Paradox of American Patriotism* (Princeton, NJ: Princeton University Press, 1999).

Political theorists and philosophers continue to debate liberal theories of political obligation. See, for example, Nancy Hirschman, *Rethinking Obligation: A Feminist Method for Political Theory* (Ithaca, NY: Cornell University Press, 1992); Patricia Smith, *Liberalism and Affirmative Obligation* (New York: Oxford University Press, 1998); and A. John Simmons, *Justification and Legitimacy: Essays on Rights and Obligations* (Cambridge: Cambridge University Press, 2001). As Linda Kerber has said, this subject has not attracted much attention from American historians, but she herself has made a signal contribution with *No Constitutional Right to Be Ladies: Women and the Obligations of Citizenship* (New York: Hill and Wang, 1998). James Mcpherson argues in *What They Fought For 1861–1864* (Baton Rouge: Louisiana State University Press, 1994) and *For Cause and Comrades: Why Men Fought in the Civil War* (New York: Oxford, 1997) that during the Civil War soldiers were motivated principally by political and ideological commitments, both liberal and republican. But in *The Vacant Chair: The Northern Soldier Leaves Home* (New York: Oxford University Press, 1993), Reid Mitchell finds a substantial mobilization of private obligations in that war similar to what I discern in World War II.

John Dower has followed up *War Without Mercy*, his seminal study of American and Japanese racial attitudes during the war, with another extraordinary book on the postwar occupation, *Embracing Defeat: Japan in the Wake of World War II* (New York: New Press, 1999). See also his *Japan in War and Peace: Selected Essays* (New York: New Press, 1993).

Norman Rockwell now has a substantial biography: Laura P. Claridge, *Norman Rockwell: A Life* (New York: Random House, 2001). Stuart Murray and James McCabe fully contextualize his *Four Freedoms* in *Norman Rockwell's Four Freedoms* (New York: Gramercy Books, 1993). Karal Ann Marling, *Norman Rockwell* (New York: Abrams, 1997), is a keen appreciation.

On the wartime experience of American families, see the fine book by William M. Tuttle Jr., *"Daddy's Gone to War": The Second World War in the Lives of America's Children* (New York: Oxford University Press, 1993). The role of American women in World War II is the subject of a large and impressive literature. Two studies of left-wing and right-wing women, respectively, that bear on the issue of political obligation are Rachel Waltner Goossen, *Women against the Good War: Conscientious Objection and Gender on the American Home Front, 1941–1947* (Chapel Hill: University of North Carolina Press, 1997); and Glen Jeansonne, *Women of the Far Right: The Mothers' Movement and World War II* (Chicago: University of Chicago Press, 1996). Betty Grable now has a pretty good, if adoring, biography: Tom McGee, *Betty Grable: The Girl with the Million Dollar Legs* (Vestal, NY: Vestal Press, 1995).

Dwight Macdonald now has a superb biography: Michael Wreszin, *A Rebel in Defense of Tradition: The Life and Politics of Dwight Macdonald* (New York: Basic Books, 1994). Wreszin has also edited an excellent selection of Macdonald's letters, *A Moral Temper: The Letters of Dwight Macdonald* (Chicago: Ivan Dee, 2001). Stephen J. Whitfield, *A Critical American: The Politics of Dwight Macdonald* (Hamden, Conn.: Archon, 1984) is solid. Gregory Sumner, *Dwight Macdonald and the "Politics" Circle: The Challenge of Cosmopolitan Democracy* (Ithaca, NY: Cornell University Press, 1996) is a fine study of the most pertinent part of Macdonald's career. Of a more limited com-pass, but nonetheless indispensable, is Robert Cummings, "Resistance and Victimiza-tion: Dwight Macdonald in the 1940s," *New Politics,* New Series 1 (1986): 213–32.

The most dated comment of all in the notes is my lament about the inadequacy of the literature on the New York Intellectuals. The subsequent twenty years have seen an outpouring of memoirs by, among others in this circle, Lionel Abel, Sidney Hook, Mary McCarthy, William Phillips, and Diana Trilling, as well as biographies and criti-cal studies of their lives and work. I will not list them all here but will note only a fine one that is especially germane to the themes of my essay: Howard Brick, *Daniel Bell and the Decline of Intellectual Radicalism: Social Theory and Political Reconciliation in the 1940s* (Madison: University of Wisconsin Press, 1986). General historical accounts now include Alexander Bloom, *Prodigal Sons: The New York Intellectuals and Their World* (New York: Oxford University Press, 1986); Terry Cooney, *The Rise of the New York Intellectuals: Partisan Review and Its Circle, 1934–1945* (Madison: University of Wisconsin Press, 1986); Neil Joumonville, *Critical Crossings: The New York Intellectu-als in Postwar America* (Berkeley: University of California Press, 1991); David Laskin, *Partisans: Marriage, Politics, and Betrayal Among the New York Intellectuals* (New York: Simon and Schuster, 2000); Harvey Teres, *Renewing the Left: Politics, Imagination, and the New York Intellectuals* (New York: Oxford University Press, 1996); and Alan Wald, *The New York Intellectuals: The Rise and Decline of the Anti-Stalinist Left from the 1930s to the 1980s* (Chapel Hill: University of North Carolina Press, 1987). See also David Hollinger, *Science, Jews, and Secular Culture: Studies in Mid–Twentieth-Century American Intellectual History* (Princeton, NJ: Princeton University Press, 1996). Hannah Arendt's thinking has become the subject of a cottage industry. For those searching for a place to begin considering the aspects of her work that I have men-tioned, I recommend Richard J. Bernstein, *Hannah Arendt and the Jewish Question* (Cambridge: MIT Press, 1996).

Debates about the responsibility of the German people for the Holocaust remain as heated as they were when Macdonald intervened in them during the spring of 1945. They took an explosive turn during the nineties with the publication of Daniel Jonah Goldhagen's *Hitler's Willing Executioners: Ordinary Germans and the Holocaust* (New York: Knopf, 1996). Goldhagen argues, *contra* Macdonald and others, that ex-terminationist anti-Semitism *was* a German folkway. Among the strongest critics of this controversial book are two historians of the Holocaust, Christopher Browning and Omer Bartov, who have themselves addressed the question in penetrating fash-ion; see Browning, *Ordinary Men: Reserve Police Battalion 101 and the Final Solution in Poland* (New York: HarperCollins, 1992); and Bartov, *Murder in Our Midst: The Holocaust, Industrial Killing, and Representation* (New York: Oxford University Press,

1996), which echoes some of Macdonald's themes. See also Robert Gellately, *Backing Hitler: Consent and Coercion in Nazi Germany* (New York: Oxford University Press, 2001); Sarah Gordon, *Hitler, Germans, and the "Jewish Question"* (Princeton, NJ: Princeton University Press, 1984); Eric A. Johnson, *Nazi Terror: The Gestapo, Jews, and Ordinary Germans* (New York: Basic Books, 1999); and Claudia Koonz, *The Nazi Conscience* (Cambridge: Harvard University Press, 2003).

Illustrations Credits

57   Revere Copper advertisement, *Life,* 20 July 1942. Courtesy Revere Copper Products, Inc.

60   Birds Eye Frosted Foods advertisement, *Life,* 29 June 1942. Courtesy of Birds Eye Foods.

63   Norman Rockwell, *Freedom of Speech,* 1943. Printed by permission of the Norman Rockwell Family Agency. Copyright © 1943, the Norman Rockwell Family Entities.

67   Betty Grable and Harry James celebrate their wedding in Las Vegas, 1945. © Hulton-Deutsch Collection/Corbis.

71   Proposed prototype for wartime advertising, 1938. Reprinted in Robert Atwan, Donald McQuade, and John Wright, eds., *Edsels, Luckies, and Frigidaires* (New York: Dell, 1979).

72   Typical World War II rape propaganda. Drawn by G. V. Lewis, reprinted in *Life,* 21 December 1942.

74   James Westbrook in his Alaska barracks, 1943. Courtesy J. C. Westbrook.

76   Betty Grable. Photograph by Frank Powolney for Twentieth Century Fox, 1941. © Bettman/Corbis.

77   Rita Hayworth. Photograph by Bob Landry, *Life,* 11 August 1941. © Bob Landry/Getty Images.

79   Sad Sack, "Back to Earth," in George Baker, *The New Sad Sack* (New York: Simon and Schuster, 1946), n.p.

81   Jane Russell admires "her" plane (1941). © Bettman/Corbis.

82   Betty Grable teaches map reading. USAAFTC, Library of Congress.

83   Palmolive Soap advertisement. Reprinted in Atwan, McQuade, and Wright, eds., *Edsels, Luckies, and Frigidaires.* Courtesy of Colgate-Palmolive Company.

85   Pin-up sent by Rita Weinberg to Bernie Kessel, *Life,* 30 November 1942.

87   Nancy (Gillam) Westbrook's homemade pin-up, Santa Maria, California, 1945. Courtesy Nancy Westbrook.

88   Lana Turner, 1941. © AP/World Wide Photos.

89   Janet "Angel" Barry, "Sweetheart of the AEF," *Life,* 30 November 1942.

90   Sailor kissing nurse in Times Square on VJ Day. Photograph by Alfred Eisenstaedt, *Life,* 27 August 1945. © Alfred Eisenstaedt/Getty Images.

92   Dwight Macdonald (1949). [Photograph by Weldon Kees?] Courtesy Dwight Macdonald Papers, Manuscripts and Archives, Yale University Library.

Index

Italicized page numbers denote illustrations.